M000079895

Praise for Swati Snacks

We are three generations of the Ambani family who cannot live without eating a meal from Swati at least once a week. Ashaben, you have given Mumbai an immense gift in institutionalising Swati Snacks over the past few decades. Here's wishing that Swati Snacks remains a timeless gift for the taste buds of many generations of Indians.

Congratulations on your book and, once again, thank you for giving us Swati Snacks in our lives.

– **Mukesh Ambani,** Chairman and MD, Reliance Industries

A Culinary Journey
of Hope and Joy

ASHA JHAVERI

WITH TANUSHKA VAID

YogiImpressions®

YogiImpressions®

SWATI SNACKS
First published in India in 2021 by
Yogi Impressions LLP
1711, Centre 1, World Trade Centre,
Cuffe Parade, Mumbai 400 005, India.
Website: www.yogiimpressions.com

First Edition, August 2021

ISBN 978-81-949674-9-1

Printed at: Thomson Press, (I) Ltd., Delhi

This book is dedicated to my loving, courageous and enterprising mother, Minakshi Jhaveri, who inspired me to follow in her footsteps.

Contents

Foreword

Love At First Bite

THIS BOOK IS A RIVETING REVELATION. AND I THOUGHT I knew everything there was to know about Swati Snacks. After all, it is not just a restaurant; it's Mumbai's beloved landmark and a must-visit destination on every tourist's itinerary.

I've been eating at Swati Snacks since 1974, when I was studying journalism in Mumbai University. Twenty years later, I wrote the first major review for Swati Snacks in my column for *The Times of India*, and since then, we have presented it with the prestigious *Times Food Award* almost every year.

In the early days, Swati Snacks at Tardeo was a no-frills restaurant. A small and simple table and chair space. But ooh! That exuberant chaat hitting the entire range of authentic flavour notes, that hand-churned ice cream with the kiss of creaminess and fruitiness... Three decades ago, it was love at first bite. And over the years, as the menu grew, so did my list of favourites. It was pure bliss to gently peel off the glistening green banana leaf to reveal the handkerchief thin, steamed rice flour panki clinging to it, to smear it with chutney, and to bite the masala mirchi. They've created several new dishes but the panki, dahi puri and freshly squeezed sugarcane juice remain its superb signatures.

Throughout the years I've known the soft-spoken Asha Jhaveri, I've requested her for many bookings in her restaurant for visiting Michelin-starred chefs, and gone to Swati several times myself to get my fix of panki and satisfy my addiction to chaat. Naturally, I was convinced that I knew all there was to know about this super popular, home-style, pure vegetarian eatery and its South Mumbai based owner; but I didn't.

Recipe For Joy

This book is a treat to beat all other treats. Not only does it share some rare recipes but Asha is also disarmingly honest about all aspects of her life. Writer Tanushka Vaid recounts Asha's life story with great insight and empathy. It is fascinating to read about the genesis of the dishes that eventually find their way into her eatery's menu and explore her early tryst with food – from how Asha, as a little girl, made the menu for her doll's marriage celebration to how she loved the rose sharbat gola on Chowpatty beach.

Along with this, is her inspirational life story of facing hardship, starting with her feisty mother who opened Swati Snacks amid huge opposition from her conservative family. In those days only the roadside bhaiyyas made chaat; so not only did Asha's mother blaze a new path, but her decision to launch Swati Snacks also symbolised women's empowerment. Equally fascinating is the story of how Asha was forced to take up the running of the restaurant after her mother's demise. Asha had never cooked before joining Swati, but voila! She would go on to open three more branches of the restaurant.

The simplicity of Swati Snacks is deceptive. The restaurant finds transcendence in dishes that seduce as well as satisfy – just like this book that you are holding in your hands. Enjoy!

Rashmi Uday Singh
Food critic, author of 40 food books

1

Hope And Joy

I WAS BORN IN 1945, TWO YEARS BEFORE THE INDEPENDENCE of India, in a small, close-knit family in Mumbai. My younger brother was born three years after me, in 1948. My parents decided to name me 'Asha' which means 'hope', and my younger brother was named 'Anand' which means 'joy'. If there were two words I could use to describe my childhood, it would be these – hope and joy. Our home was always filled with warmth, laughter, and love. Being born so close to India's independence, we were raised in a society steeped in traditional Indian values, with some elements of European influence seeping through, especially when it came to food and local cuisine.

Our home was in an area called Gowalia Tank, which was a hub of the Gujarati-Jain community in South Mumbai. Gowalia Tank had three lanes that met in a central circle. We lived on Alexandra road, while my *nana-nani* lived a five-minute walk away on Laburnum road. The area was always relaxed and peaceful – full of

1

greenery and the quiet murmur of life passing by. In those days, there were no loud horns blaring or tires screeching. The loud noises, if any, were of children's laughter and cheer when schools got over for the day.

The surrounding locality had a Jain temple, two schools, and small restaurants and shops nestled within it. It was like a world of its own, and for many years, my life revolved around the people and places within these three lanes.

In our childhood, Anand and I spent a lot of time at our nana and nani's place, which was like a second home for us. On weekends and holidays especially, we would go to their home in the morning and stay there till lunch. Though we loved both our grandparents, their personalities were poles apart. While our nana was strict and adamant about following rules, our nani was easygoing and had a more friendly relationship with us.

Our nani was a staunch follower of Jainism, and from a young age she tried to inculcate in me the importance of prayer and rituals. Every Sunday morning, I used to go to her home dressed in my finest, and we would walk together to the local Jain temple, a short five-minute walk away in a nearby lane. I have many fond memories of those walks; it was a time when I used to feel that there was no one else in the world except the two of us and I had her undivided attention.

On the other hand, even as a little boy, Anand was not religiously inclined, seemingly taking after our mother in that regard. He never accompanied us on these visits and though our nani tried hard to persuade him, he never relented.

Our nani taught me many *shlokas*, some of which I continued to recite for many years even after my marriage. One of the first shlokas I learnt was the *Navkar Mantra* and I have a distinct memory of my nani and I praying together with our hands clasped, and eyes squeezed shut, convinced that the Gods were listening to our every word.

Is School Over, Yet?

If there was one dent in my otherwise happy, peaceful life, it was school. To say I disliked school as much as the school disliked me would not be an exaggeration.

Until Class 6, Anand and I went to a Gujarati-medium school called Sahkari Vidya Mandir at Tardeo, a 15-minute drive from home. When I failed my Class 6 examinations in mathematics and science, and was told to repeat the year, my mother refused, and transferred us to different schools.

Anand started attending New Era School and I went to Fellowship School, both of which were just a five-minute walk from our home. Though they were both co-education schools, we were separated intentionally. Since I was evidently not good at studies, my mother was worried that I would keep failing, and a day might come that Anand and I end up in the same class, though I was three years older than him. To avoid this embarrassment

3

and the repercussions it could have, she set us out on different paths.

To add to my misery, the new school was a combination of both English and Gujarati mediums. The introduction of English as not only a subject, but also the medium of instruction for other subjects, seemed like an impossible challenge for me. I found it very difficult to keep up with what was happening in class and I spent a lot of time staring fixatedly at my book, willing myself not to cry.

My weakest subject was mathematics. I couldn't calculate in my head or recite the times tables from memory. The numbers would swarm around on the page in front of me while I helplessly tried to make sense of them.

Some of my worst memories and fears stem from those days in the classroom. I was constantly yelled at by my teachers for being slow; they would think that I was stupid and would never amount to anything. I would often be made to stand on the bench for getting the answers wrong – head hanging in shame, and cheeks burning with embarrassment.

I used to stare at the clock, day after day, praying that the school bell would ring and I could run away to the safety of my home. I remember being scared and feeling that no matter what I did, I was just not good enough.

The only respite I got from the long hours at school was that during every recess and lunch break I could walk back home to eat before returning back for the remainder of the lessons, and my brother would do the same. Back in the comfort of my home, I was able to take some deep breaths and relax.

Whenever we went to our nani's home, and I told her that my teachers didn't think I would amount to anything in life, she would shake her head and smile lovingly. Brushing my hair gently, she would say, "Don't worry Asha. It's okay. You will be all right." Her simple words filled with love and support meant the whole world to me and gave me the courage to return to school day after day.

Children Of The World

I had a small but close group of friends with whom I spent most of my time either in the school canteen or the compound of my building. Our school canteen was famous for its sandwiches, *samosas* and *ragda patties*. I would get twenty rupees per month as pocket money and used it sparingly to make sure that I never fell short of it and could go for outings with my friends.

My friends would get similar amounts of pocket money and in an effort to save it, they would often accompany me home instead of going out, and we would spend many hours together laughing, talking, and playing games. If Anand and his friends joined us, we would become a large, boisterous group, running around the house until we were sent down to the building compound where we would play games like kho-kho, saakli, hide-n-seek and catch-n-cook.

At any given evening, the sound of laughter and

screaming children always penetrated the walls of neighbouring houses, filling our community with love, joy, and the occasional shout to 'tone it down!'

One of my fondest memories is when my friend and I decided to get our dolls married. I had a girl doll and she had a boy doll. Together we planned an elaborate wedding ceremony replete with traditional customs and a fancy menu.

The ceremony was held at my house and was a lavish affair for us. The wedding had a large guest list, and all of our friends from school were invited. After the wedding rituals were performed by us, looking like very serious, naïve little girls, we served the food.

This was the first time in my life I had ever designed a menu and I left no stone unturned. My friend and I had asked our mothers to cook us some food, and now it lay spread out for everyone to share. We had homemade hot *jalebis*, Gujarati *meethi dal* with white rice, *aloo ki sukhi sabzi*, *dahi vadas*, white *dhoklas* and potato chips. Later that evening, everyone left our home feeling very impressed with the food they had eaten and the wedding they had witnessed.

As children we made up many such events and our parents always indulged us. In those days, we didn't have technology to distract us, or rash drivers to endanger us. We had space and time and freedom.

Our parents didn't worry about our safety or pressure us about the future – they simply didn't have to. Our parents didn't raise us to be scared of the world; they raised us as if we were children of the world.

Oh, Brother!

As children, Anand and I had a maid called Radhabai, who would accompany us everywhere. One of the places she frequently took us to was Chowpatty beach, one of the largest beaches in South Mumbai, and a 15-minute drive from our home.

Amongst the many hawkers, there was a *golawala* who would come there and sell *golas* of different colours. Anand and I weren't allowed to eat food from outside very often, and especially not golas, which were considered very questionable in terms of hygiene. The vendor would garnish each gola with a few masalas like *chaat masala* that would add a salty, tangy flavour. I used to love licking the masala off the gola and frequently asked him to add some extra masala to it. My favourite flavour was the 'kala khatta gola' that got its name from the kala khatta sharbat that was used. It had a combination of sweet and sour taste, and was perfect for hot summer days. The golas would make my lips look coloured too and after eating them I could pretend as if I was a grown-up woman with lipstick on. So whenever I wanted my lips to look red, I would have the 'rose sharbat gola' or the 'orange sharbat gola'.

Radhabai knew about this and would secretly buy them for me against my mother's wishes. Anand, on the other hand, never bought a gola or ate anything from outside unless he was allowed. He was a quiet boy who always listened to what he was told. This was just one of the differences between us.

Anand and I were poles apart at almost everything, from the food we liked, to the way we spoke or dressed. Nothing in us seemed to match. The biggest difference, however, was that while I barely managed to pass in school, my brother was a genius. He was intelligent, hardworking and cleared his exams with flying colours. Growing up, this filled me with a lot of insecurity and I always thought my mother loved him better. This made me feel quite jealous and I often took it out on him.

Taking advantage of my position as a big sister, I would often bully him into doing what I wanted. Whenever we had disagreements, I would fight and sometimes even hit him. Though he held his own in all fights, being older than him, I would usually win.

When we entered our teens, however, our relationship started to change. We stopped fighting over little things and grew closer, the way most siblings eventually do.

One of the incidents that showed how deeply Anand cared about me was when I was around thirteen years old. Anand, Viralalji (who was officially our cook, though he was almost like family to us) and I had gone cycling to Worli (a suburb of Mumbai). On our way back, we were cycling on Peddar Road (around half-way between our home and Worli)—and this was when the flyover connecting Peddar Road to Hughes Road hadn't been built yet—so there was just one steep slope of around 500m between Peddar Road and Worli. I don't know what came over me, but I decided to cycle down the slope at breakneck speed just to see how fast I could go. The problem, I soon realised, was that I didn't know how to use the breaks properly and so lost control over my cycle as I sped down the road. I could hear Anand and Viralalji screaming behind me, saying, "Asha press the break!" but I was frozen to my seat. Fortunately, when the road straightened out, my cycle slowed down automatically and as soon as I got off, Anand came running from behind, screaming, "You could have been hurt! Why don't you take care of yourself?" Though I didn't say anything to him back then, I secretly thought that it was worth it, since now I knew that Anand cared much more about me than he would ever admit.

Though we didn't have long, heart-to-heart talks, or share secrets with each other, I always knew I could count on him to be my pillar of strength whenever I needed it. Over time, I stopped viewing him as my 'annoying little brother' and started to recognise him as my equal and as my friend through life.

2

The Touch Of Love

FOOD WAS ALWAYS A CENTRAL PART OF MY LIFE WHILE growing up, and a prominent feature at all family events and festivals. We would traditionally have specific combinations of Gujarati sweets, *namkeens* and main courses that worked well together and we rarely changed them. For example, *undhiya* was eaten with *puris, val ni dal,* and jalebi, *shrikhand* or *shiro* as dessert. Another combination was *chola* and *sambhariya potatoes* eaten with puris and a dessert called *lapsi.* The food was usually prepared at home with the women of the household lovingly preparing it for the rest of the family. My mother was an exceptional cook and famous among her friends for the dishes she would make.

When my mother got married, they had a house help called Viralal Raval. Gradually she started to teach him how to cook, and soon he had taken over the cooking for the entire household. After that, my mother would only cook on special occasions or for trying out new recipes, and as children, we were always taught to refer to Viralalji as our *maharaj*.

In our home, the social barriers between the working class and us were blurred, and we were taught to treat everyone with respect and dignity. Our staff was never considered to be beneath us, but instead, treated as members of the family. This enriched our interactions with them and proved beneficial for all of us; while they would get a home away from home, we would get support and loyalty for life.

I loved eating Punjabi cuisine and my favourite dishes were *vegetable do pyaza, kali dal, onion kulcha* or *pudina paratha* and vegetable biryani with *raita*. I also had a sweet tooth for vanilla ice cream with hot chocolate sauce, and caramel custard that we would get from a local restaurant. Anand, on the other hand, enjoyed a more traditional palate. His favourite dish was a combination of steamed white rice, *Gujarati toor dal* with *ghee*, green coriander chutney and *papads*. Surprisingly, neither of us was too fond of *chaats*, though our mother was famous for making them.

Since we had a maharaj who would cook up delicacies for us daily, we were always taught the value of hot, home-cooked meals, and how to appreciate the people who were cooking them. Another habit stressed upon at home was to eat everything, and not be picky about our food habits. We always had a sufficient helping of green vegetables, pulses, and curd with every meal.

While occasionally, at our home, we could bully our way into getting food we wanted, this was not the case at our nana's home. My nana was very strict. In order to help us learn how to eat all kinds of food, he would serve us different vegetables every time we went there and foods like *karela, doodhi* and *gunda* were staples at his house.

As young children, my brother and I were not too fond of those vegetables, but being scared of our nana, we couldn't say anything, and quietly ate whatever was placed before us. This strict upbringing had the desired effect on our food habits, and till today I can eat almost all vegetables with perfect equanimity.

There was a belief in ancient India that the taste of the food depended not only on the ingredients and recipe used, but also on the emotions that the chef prepared it with. By treating our staff with respect and in raising us to believe in equality of labour, my mother ensured that everyone who came in contact with our food did so with love and goodness in their hearts.

Though my mother never expressly said anything, I believe that this 'touch of love' was the secret to the special taste of our homemade food, and the reason why everyone got up from the dining table feeling satisfied and blessed.

The Flower Blooms

My mother always made sure that my brother and I were well exposed to the world outside, and so, we often went for holidays to different places in India. When I was 11 years old, we made a trip to Ooty, a hill station in Southern India, during the summer of 1956. It was Anand, my mother, her friends with their children, and me. There were nine of us, and we went for two weeks.

We travelled by an overnight train since planes were not as popular yet, and found the journey almost as exciting as the destination. We loved seeing the landscapes pass outside our window, running around in the train compartments or striking up spontaneous friendships with other children during the long hours.

On that trip, we went not just to Ooty but also to surrounding cities such as Mysore, Chennai, and Bangalore.

To say that the natural beauty in Ooty was astounding would be an understatement. Everywhere we looked, there was Mother Nature at Her finest. The hills were covered in a carpet of green and wild flowers sprang from the bushes in the ground. The sky was covered in streaks of white and blue, and the view of the rising sun from our hotel window added vibrant splashes of orange and red to the sky, as if God Himself had picked up His brush and decided to paint. During that idyllic trip, we would wake up with the call of the birds and sleep to the lullaby of the insects hovering around the Ratrani flowers. I had thought my home in Mumbai to be peaceful, but it was nothing compared to this.

We would try out some local cuisine in every city, and since we were in South India, *dosa* was the staple everywhere. In Ooty, I had a dosa for the first time and immediately fell in love with it. It was also the first time I saw how one dish was reimagined in so many different ways. While the dosa was thicker in Chennai, it was thinner in Bangalore. The taste of the chutney and *sambhar* also varied in flavour and consistency. We would eagerly wait to try out this dish in different places so that we could compare our thoughts on it and rate the food accordingly — this had become our little holiday game.

One of the highlights of the trip was a visit to the flower show at the Ooty Government Botanical Gardens. The annual event was often referred to as the 'Showstopper of the South' and having witnessed it, I can definitely vouch for it.

Rows upon rows of flowers were lined up in a vibrant display of colours. Flowers of every colour, shape and size, including local plants and exotic variants were grown throughout the year especially for this occasion. It would take us a few hours to walk through the entire garden, but we hardly realised it because it was like walking through the gardens of heaven. While we children ran ahead, marvelling at the diverse colours, the adults lingered behind, to appreciate the delicate intricacies of the flora.

That day I saw the Dahlia flower in all its glory; its pinkish-purple majestic wonder etched in my memory for years to come. And one day, several years later, when I decided to try my hand at sketching, the same Dahlia would come to mind.

For a long time, my mother had been trying to figure out what I could do after I completed school. Since I was not good at studies, pursuing a typical higher education degree didn't make sense for someone like me. When she saw my sketch of the Dahlia flower, she discovered that I had a hidden aptitude for art and she enrolled me in the JJ School of Arts.

My journey through college began in 1962 – six years after my first glimpse of the Dahlia flower. And unlike in school, where I felt like a seed desperately trying to push its way through the soil to reach the sun and air; in college, I would find the perfect environment to finally bloom.

3

Prepare For Take Off

AROUND THE SAME TIME, MY MOTHER'S CHAATS HAD BEEN steadily rising in popularity with relatives and friends. She would make them during special occasions or when we had guests come over. More and more people started encouraging her to start selling her chaats commercially. They believed that this was just the item Mumbai had been waiting for, and that people would come in droves to get their share of tasty home-cooked chaats at good rates. The idea started to take root in my mother's mind and she decided to test it out.

If her friends had thought that getting my mother to agree to this idea was hard, they didn't know what lay ahead. My parents had separated when I was six years old, so the decision to start a new venture should have been entirely hers. But instead, she faced strong opposition from her family every step of the way. While a few relatives had been open to and supportive of the idea, most of them were against it.

16

Her family was aghast at her decision to start selling chaats and didn't spare any opportunity to remind her of the implications. We were from a conventional Jain family and this idea came as a shock for all.

In those days, the notion of a working woman was highly unusual in our community. Most women would stay at home, look after the household, and have their cooking limited to serving the members of the family. This was the image of a traditional daughter-in-law in people's minds. Usually, it was only a male member like the husband or father who could be the breadwinner, and if a woman decided to work, it signified that the men were not able to earn enough to provide for the family. In such circumstances, many opposed my mother's desire to work, fearful of the message that it would send out.

The greater point of contention, however, was that my mother was planning to sell chaat. In those days, no restaurant served chaat, which was seen as street food. Selling chaat was associated with the image of *bhaiyyas* carrying food and stands on their heads, moving from place to place in the hope of earning enough money to send back home to their native place. Our family was financially stable, and they didn't understand why my mother would want to portray an image so different from ours. They thought that it would harm the reputation of the family, to be seen doing something considered very 'lowly' in our society.

As children, we often heard all these criticisms being hurled at our mother, but we weren't very concerned. Every time they said something, we would look at our mother to see if she was taking it well. We knew that as long she seemed all right, we would be all right too – that there was nothing to be worried or scared about. And she always did take it well.

Though my mother was respectful of their concerns, she did not pay any heed to them. She was a determined, strong woman, and once she had taken a decision, there was no backing down. She fought against all the negativity and pessimism that was directed at her; not with words or pain, but with her actions.

My mother never thought that it was anyone else's right to tell her what to do or how to live her life. Even in a conservative society where there was so much emphasis on conforming to perceptions of the perfect daughter or daughter-in-law, she never let go of herself and of who she was, beyond the boundaries of the roles she had to play.

While people tried to pull her down, she started to work silently, resolutely, to build herself up, accumulating all the strength and power she knew she had, much like how the engine of a plane gears up before hitting the runway. And then, she took off, taking all of us with her.

Swati Is Born

When my nana and nani realised that my mother was not going to change her mind, they decided to help her, as this way they could be a part of her journey and make it easier for her. My nani gave my mother the initial investment of Rs.35,000 with which she could purchase a small place of around 250 square feet at Tardeo. Though this space could accommodate only four tables seating 12 people at one time, it was chosen because of the convenience of its location. Tardeo was only a 15-minute drive away from our home, and hence, easily accessible at all times.

My mother decided to call the place 'Swati Snacks', which was surprising since neither my mother (whose name was Minakshi) nor anyone else in the family was called Swati. The menu had different chaat items such as *pani puri, dahi puri* made with fresh curd, *sev puri* and *ragda patties* served with a side of green chutney. Swati was officially launched on 31 December 1962, a symbolic day for us because it marked the end of age-old ideals regarding a woman's role in our family, and ushered in the start of many new adventures.

The initial customers were friends and relatives of the family, but word soon spread and many people from the local Jain-Gujarati community started pouring in. Swati was a pure vegetarian restaurant and provided a common place for families to gather since they knew there would be something to everyone's liking.

What made Swati different was that my mother started it as a hobby and not as a business. Though she used to sell chaats and generate income the way a business does, her motive was not to make profit but to serve the food she loved, to the people she loved. She always used the choicest ingredients and added her special 'touch of love' to all the dishes.

She started to become famous because people knew that here was a woman from a reputed family who was creating exceptional quality of food for family and friends with no desire to cheat them. They started to view Swati as a place that would serve food similar to their home-cooked food in terms of hygiene, but with much better taste. This was her trademark.

My mother and Viralal maharaj would start preparing all the chaat items at home in the morning. Everything, from the *puris* of pani puri to the *sev* of sev puri — all of which were bought ready-made by most restaurants because of the sheer effort it took to make them — were handmade from scratch, and what was more, the leftovers from the previous day were given away and never reused. This level of attention to detail and quality was very unusual and it reflected in the food. Customers always remarked that even if there were similar chaats on offer by other vendors in Mumbai, you could tell if a dish was from Swati simply by looking at it.

After the preparations were made each morning, our house help, Devji, would take the food in a taxi and head over to the restaurant by 1:00 p.m. He would arrange the tables neatly, clean the place, and perform small tasks until my mother and maharaj would open the restaurant and join him. Swati used to be open to customers from 3:00 p.m. to 10:00 p.m. on all days.

In the evening, maharaj would come back home to cook dinner for Anand and me, and then we would wrap up the dinner in a tiffin box and take it to my mother at Swati. We would often stay back with her till closing time and come home together.

One of the unique items she started serving in Swati was hand-churned ice cream. The churner was a wooden container with an aluminium jar in the centre. She would boil fresh milk and put it in the aluminium jar and fill the sides of the jar with ice and rock salt. Once the milk was cooled, she would add the fresh or dry fruits (such as *sithaphal, kesar pista*, strawberries or oranges) and sugar, and start churning the machine by hand.

In the process of churning, the milk would become thick like ice cream, but would remain soft, have the freshness of fruits, and not the frozen taste of regular ice creams. The introduction of this hand-churned ice cream was seen as a sophisticated alternative to regular frozen treats. Word spread quickly about the delicious hand-churned ice creams and it wasn't long before we realised that the four tables at Swati could no longer accommodate the large crowds.

Since there weren't enough funds for expansion, my mother decided to start serving people in their cars. This turned out to be immensely popular as people could come, pick up the food and eat to their heart's content, without leaving the comfort of their cars.

Swati was the first non-roadside place to serve what was traditionally considered as street food, and what her family had felt would be an embarrassment, turned out to be her greatest strength.

The lack of formal, organised places to eat chaat, made Swati stand out as a diamond amongst rocks, and people started to come from far and near. Since the matter of hygiene and quality were taken care of, families with young and old members alike could eat the food without worrying about falling ill, which would usually happen by eating roadside chaat that used poor quality ingredients and water.

Before long, my mother's friends and extended family started to heap praises on what a good job she was doing, and how her business was growing well. Slowly but surely, the family that had questioned her ability to be successful, started to realise that in a matter of a few months, she already was. And those who said she would bring shame to the family, now turned proudly to friends and family alike, to boast about how well she was doing.

For my mother, it wasn't so much the money or the praise that affected her – neither had been the objective for starting the business. She never fell into the trap of taking shortcuts with quality or quantity after she had made a name for herself and instead, continued to provide the best on a platter.

Even once the money started to flow in, she never once let the fruits of her success blindside her from her goals. What mattered most to her was that she could share her joy of cooking and provide people a place like home to eat. This was her only mission and this was what helped Swati to continue rising in popularity.

4

Life Carries On Smoothly

IN THE MEANTIME, IN EARLY 1962, THE SAME YEAR THAT Swati was launched, I started my college life at the JJ School of Arts at Fort, a 20-minute drive from my home. I enrolled in the House Decoration class where we had to paint, sketch or draw different subjects such as 'door', 'sofa' or other house decoration items.

My mother had been correct when she recognised my talent through my sketch of the Dahlia flower, and I did have a strong aptitude for the arts. I found a friend in a girl called Sadhana in my class and over the course of the next three years, Sadhana or I would come first and second alternatively in college examinations and bag the scholarships for the rest of the year. With the scholarships I won, my tuition over there was almost free.

Sadhana soon became my best friend and we started another practice: for one month, I used to carry lunch every day for both of us from home, and the next month she would carry lunch for us. We would follow this pattern for the entire year.

My favourite dishes from her house were *bread-dhokla* and *moong ka kadhi*, which her mother used to make. She loved eating most of my home-cooked food too. Her favourite items were *bhindi ki sabzi, Gujarati khatta-meetha dal*, and *drumstick ki sabzi* eaten with *roti* or white rice. Once a week, we would also go to a local restaurant called Gaylord and feast on the buttery, grilled cheese sandwiches and hot coffee. The arrangement worked very well for both of us. This, along with the work I was exposed to, made college an exciting and wonderful time in my life and I graduated from JJ School of Arts at the top of my class in 1965.

The Start Of My Married Life

The same year, as I turned 20 years old, I got married into a traditional Jain joint family.

One of the most vivid memories I have from the wedding is of Anand crying as he held my hand during my *bidai*. In that one moment, I knew that no matter what, we would always have each other to fall back on. I knew that that picture would always be etched in my heart – the picture of a young girl and her even younger brother standing together on the cusp of life, unwilling to face life without each other.

Until this time, though my mother had been so passionate about cooking, I had never lifted a finger to make even a cheese sandwich or a piece of toast. This meant that when I got married I had to learn everything, including the basics of cutting vegetables, from scratch. My mother-in-law was a great source of help and comfort for me, and she patiently taught me all that I didn't know, showering me with love and encouragement every step of the way. She treated me like her own daughter and loved me the way only a mother could.

There were many adjustments to be made in this new life. I had come from a small three-member family and this was a large family of 20 people. While I had grown up seeing my mother work and be independent, over here, women fulfilled the traditional roles of being a housewife and mother. I had grown up like a princess, having things done for me by others, and in my new house I was expected to pull my weight and contribute just like everyone else. These changes seemed like too many and too fast, but slowly and steadily I started to adjust and settle down in this new routine.

I still kept up with my love for painting, and over the course of the next few years, from 1974 to 1981, I held seven exhibitions of my artworks. Six of them were held at the art gallery at Taj Hotel, Mumbai, and one was held in Delhi. I would rent out the hall at these galleries and put up an exhibition for at least four days. During this time, friends, family, regular customers, and general visitors would drop by and browse through the collection on display. Many of my paintings sold immediately and I would cherish the feeling of knowing that my artworks would be a part of someone's home or office for years to come.

My favourite subject to paint was Mother Nature in all Her different forms. The themes I chose included flowers, scenery, and birds – sometimes individually, and at other times all-together. My artwork on birds, in which I portrayed local and exotic birds in a new light, was widely appreciated.

One of my favourite paintings was the portrait of an eagle. I still have a vivid memory of the textures and colours used to create it, and after looking at it, many buyers would ask me to start devoting all my free time to painting since I had such an aptitude for it.

However, painting wasn't my profession, it was just my hobby, and I was content to leave it that way. Besides, the duties of being a daughter-in-law such as cooking all our meals, taking care of the ageing members of the family and keeping a check on household expenses prevented me from indulging in any other activity full-time.

Swati – My Mother's Third Baby

While I had been busy settling into a new life, my mother had taken Swati to greater heights and expanded the restaurant by purchasing the shop next door so that it could accommodate 40 people at once. She had introduced items like *pav bhaji, missal pav,* and Indian-style pizzas, and got more staff on board by training our house help to cook, just as she had done with Viralalji.

Swati was even featured in the *Illustrated Weekly* – a famous news magazine – and *Femina India* – a leading women's magazine of the time. Locals, people coming from the suburbs of Mumbai, and tourists visiting from different cities, all made sure to drop by and taste the food that was making waves in culinary circles all over the city.

Many of my relatives from my husband's side of the family would ask me to convince my mother to sell Swati to them so that they could reap its good fortunes. But my mother would not relent. Swati was her third baby, and she was fiercely, and rightfully, protective of it. I, on the other hand, was happy in my own world, and had never looked at or considered joining it. Soon, this was all about to change.

5

End Of An Era

LIFE HAD BEEN PROGRESSING SMOOTHLY AND PREDICTABLY for many years. My mother had diabetes but she would take her medicines and insulin regularly and it was never a cause for concern. On 16 October 1979, a few days before my 34th birthday, my mother had a severe diabetes attack. She passed away within two days, at the young age of 53. Everything happened very suddenly; her life was taken away from her, from us, in the blink of an eye and I spent the next few days in shock, trying to process what had happened.

There had been no forewarning, no time to say goodbye. There were only unsaid words, unheard stories, and a lifetime of memories. There were memories of her grace and strength and joy, of her warm hugs and wide smiles and tender kisses. Memories that I would hold on to forever like a child hugs their favourite blanket close for comfort in moments of struggle or fear.

Soon, the practical aspects started to overtake the

emotional ones – the biggest challenge being what we would do about Swati. Our mother had looked after Swati on her own with no help from Anand or me. We had never spoken about who would take over the restaurant after her, simply because the event of her passing had seemed far away in the future. Now, this question loomed before us, occupying our thoughts in all our waking moments. There was no shortage of people willing to buy Swati, but Anand and I knew that our mother had never wanted to sell it, and we wanted to honour her wish. We knew that somehow or the other, Swati must remain with us.

Anand had shifted to Ahmedabad almost a decade earlier and was raising a family of his own over there, so the question of his shifting back to Mumbai and leaving his business to look after the restaurant didn't arise. All heads started to turn to me, looking at me as the prospective heir to Swati. Far from being happy about it, I considered this as another unfair act of life – my mother being taken away and then saddling me with a business I had no idea how to run.

Anand tried to talk me into it, saying that even our mother didn't have any experience when she started. But, I reasoned, at least she had passion. I had never been interested in cooking food; in fact, I disliked having to spend any time in the kitchen. The thought of going to Swati every day filled me with fear and uncertainty.

However, one day, when my nani called me up, and told me to at least try and handle Swati till we could come up with a better plan, I knew I couldn't refuse my fate any longer; I had never been able to say 'no' to her.

I had remarried a few years earlier into a more liberal family, and my husband, Sailesh, was very open-minded about the prospect of me going to work. He was supportive and encouraged me to start going to Swati to help my family out.

The first time I went to Swati as its new owner was in December 1979, two months after my mother passed away. I remember feeling like I was back in school – a fish out of water – desperately staring at the clock and willing the hands to move faster so that I could go back home. It was only due to our childhood maharaj Viralalji's conviction in my abilities that I continued to go back every day. He would tell me, "Don't worry, I am there for you; you will learn everything. Together, we will keep Swati running."

Initially, I started going to Swati only for a few hours on Sundays. Sailesh would drop me in the evening and then pick me up at night. During other days of the week, I would just stop by the restaurant for 10-15 minutes, running out of there at the first opportunity I got.

There wasn't anything specific for me to do at Swati in terms of my job profile. The staff knew their individual responsibilities and the restaurant would run on its own like clockwork. Besides, I was too caught up in my own grief to want to proactively do something on my own. For almost one year it was this way – I would just go and sit at Swati because it was obligatory for me to do so, but I thought I was making no real contribution.

The entire credit for handling and maintaining the restaurant during that period goes to Viralalji, and Devji, our house help-turned-cook. They looked after all the aspects including buying quality ingredients, hiring staff, and looking after the customers. They would give me the money from the sales of the previous day when I would go to the restaurant the following day. The love and respect my mother had shown them throughout her life were never forgotten and they repaid her by helping our family get through this difficult period.

The staff, led by Viralalji and Devji, had ample opportunities to cut corners or to cheat, but the thought of doing so never once crossed their minds. My mother had always made them feel as if Swati was their baby too, and the responsibility they had to look after this baby properly weighed heavily on their minds.

Throughout this transition period, the customers of Swati didn't find any change in the taste or perfection of the food; and buoyed by the love of the staff working behind the scenes, Swati continued to maintain its reputation and high standards.

I believe that this gift of loyal staff built up through decades, was my mother's last gift to us. It was her final bow before the curtains closed, symbolising the end of an era, not just for us, but also in the legacy of Swati.

6

New Life, Newer Responsibilities

AFTER MARRIAGE, SAILESH AND I HAD A TRADITION OF going to the theatre to see plays on Sundays. Sometimes it would be just the two of us, and at other times we would go with our common friends. Either way, the evening was spent watching plays and going for dinner. He would drop me off at Swati for a few hours in the afternoon and then come pick me up so that we could reach the theatre on time. Since Sailesh worked during the rest of the week, we looked forward to these few precious hours together.

Towards the end of 1980, a year after my mother's passing, Viralalji saw that I had started to settle down in Swati and had become familiar with the staff and regular customers. He thought that it was time to start giving me more responsibility around the restaurant instead of the mere titular role I had till then. He was like a father figure for me, gently prodding me to stand up, take charge of my life, and take charge of Swati.

With this in mind, Viralalji came up to me and said,

"Asha, now you have to give up your Sundays and start dedicating your free time to Swati. Sundays are workdays for us, they are not holidays." He suggested that I could sit on the cash counter and handle the money coming in.

The idea of sitting on the cash counter the entire day was terrifying for me. Not only was I reluctant to give up my Sundays, but also I was sure that I would not be able to keep track of the money and would make mistakes in the change that had to be given back. Mathematics had always been my weakest subject, and while I had thought that I had left it behind in school, it was making an entry again in my life.

My parents-in-law were against the idea of me going to work full-time on Sunday. They would argue that since Sailesh had only one day off from work, I should spend that day with him. They said that I could go to work any other day of the week and should not compromise on the little time Sailesh and I got to spend together.

I had many discussions with them over the course of the next few days. Since Sundays were the busiest days at Swati, Viralalji needed my help in handling the cash and crowds; I explained that while this was not the best option, it seemed to be our only one, and soon they reluctantly agreed to have me try it out.

Sailesh was very cooperative and agreed to give up our day together so that I could pay more attention to Swati. Since we had only one car, he would drop me off in the afternoon and then come pick me up again at 10 p.m. when the restaurant would close. Every minute spent at Swati felt like an eternity, and I was sure that the day would end in sheer embarrassment for me when people realised that I would fumble even with the basic calculations required on the cash counter.

In those days calculators weren't easily available and every time the waiters gave me the customer's money, I would hide my hands under the desk, silently trying to count on my fingers the amount of change I was required to give back. I would try being as inconspicuous as I could, hoping that no one would realise that I still calculated like a primary school girl.

The impatient faces of the customers waiting to get their money made my heart beat so fast that I thought it would burst out of my chest. Their annoyed sigh or the sound of their fingers tapping the desk when they realised they weren't getting their change back within a second, made me so nervous that I often forgot my counting and had to start from scratch.

I would have run away the first day itself if it weren't for Viralalji constantly reassuring me that I would get better over time and that he was always there for me.

Gradually my parents-in-law also started coming by every Sunday to sit and eat at Swati. Their favourite dish was missal pav and they would look forward to their weekly outings. Even our friends, with whom we would initially go to watch plays, started coming to Swati for dinner, adding more love and laughter to the already packed restaurant. Their presence at Swati made my time there easier, and one by one, the days started to fly by.

While I did eventually get better at being at the cash register, I was never completely comfortable calculating on the spot. Thankfully, in a few years calculators would make the necessity of having that skill redundant. What would never be redundant, however, would be learning how to face my biggest fears, how to pursue excellence, and how to show loving compassion to others as they overcame hurdles in their own lives.

Buy Smart, Sell Smarter

By 1981, two years after I first started, I was finally comfortable in my new role and gradually started to notice irregularities in the way Swati was being run. While my mother was alive, Swati had always been a hobby for her and she didn't pay much attention to the small details of day-to-day operations – all of this was left to Viralalji and Devji. However, as I started to get interested in Swati and noticed these mistakes, I knew that it was time to make some changes.

Until that time, all the vegetables had been sourced from local, roadside vendors. Viralalji tried to get the best deal he could, but since he often purchased from retail vendors, the discounts were few, and costs kept rising. When I mentioned this to my father-in-law, he said that his driver would be able to help.

Babubhai, his driver, was very well connected in the working class circles of Mumbai, and he recommended going to the market at Byculla (a 25-minute drive away from Swati), and getting their quotations on different vegetables. Once we were there, he put me in touch with a vendor and we worked out a deal that would give us the same vegetables at almost half the cost we were being supplied at earlier. We were elated with this deal because we knew that these drastic drops in prices freed up the money that could now be used in other areas.

Similarly, even when it came to buying grains or spices, we switched over to wholesalers instead of retailers, to benefit from the price differences. Locating and negotiating with these dealers was difficult, but we knew that despite the initial effort it took, it would be worth it in the long run.

Sailesh's friend was the owner of Status restaurant, a popular eatery serving South Indian food, and I would frequently consult him about matters of purchase and sale. I would show him the quotations I was getting for different vegetables, pulses, and spices, and he would tell me when I was getting a fair deal and when I was being cheated.

It turned out that though I thought we were getting good deals because they were lesser than the prices of retailers, they were still high as compared with other wholesalers. We couldn't believe that we were still purchasing at higher prices than others and were determined to get our money's worth.

Armed with this new information, we went back to the market and fiercely negotiated with the vendors for many days.

Another thing that caused these negotiations to be tricky was that we were never willing to compromise on quality. We wanted the freshest produce from the most verified sources and we wanted the best deal for it. What we were asking for was not unreasonable since they did quote better rates to their more experienced customers. It was just that since they could see we were new to the field, they wanted to make the most they could from the deal. While I could understand their way of thinking, I knew that I was responsible for getting the best bargain for us.

In the end, though we got the deals we needed, the entire process was tiring and confusing for us because we were new to this level of bargaining. However, this was a major hurdle that we tackled and as a result, without increasing the prices of our dishes, we managed to sharply increase our profits by cutting down on our costs.

All Hands On Deck

Another aspect of the business that was eating into our funds was that initially we used to employ part-time waiters. These waiters would work in other restaurants till 6 p.m. and then come to Swati. They were unreliable in terms of their work ethic and timings, and were often late to work or would come in no mood to give their best. It was a constant source of worry to us, for we had to make sure that we were not short-staffed or being cheated by the ones we did have because they were not giving us their best. We would keep one eye on the clock, waiting for them to come on time so that the other members of the staff would not be overburdened. One day, I had had enough and told Viralalji that we would not wait for them any longer.

We decided to replace everyone who came late or

didn't show up for work, clearing out more than half our staff as a strong warning to others to shape up or move out. We kept up this practice of frequently removing staff for a few months, retaining only those who were efficient and passionate about working for and with us.

This was a major step for me. I had always been fearful of people judging me or thinking that I didn't know what I was doing if I went against them. However, as my courage built up through months of running Swati, I was confident enough to take this decision and not worry about how others would perceive me. Viralalji supported me on this and helped in outing the waiters who misbehaved or tried to manipulate us.

A major problem with the part-time waiters was that many of them would spare no opportunity to steal money. The system was that waiters would keep track of the orders on their tables and report it to me at the cash counter at the end of the meal. There was no formal system of billing and the waiters would just make a mental note of the dishes ordered, give me the money collected and take back the change required. The tips they got were to be put in a central jar from which it would be distributed equally among all waiters at the end of the month. This was what was supposed to happen.

What actually happened was that waiters often lied about the dishes ordered, giving us only some money and pocketing the rest. No one could prove that more money had been collected than they reported since they were the only ones keeping track of the orders at their table. They would hide the tips they got in their shoes or socks, rarely depositing anything in the central jar, but were always eager to take their share from it when the month got over.

Fed up with this system and the money we were losing, I hired another person to sit at the cash counter with me. Together, we would keep writing down the orders going to different tables and instruct the waiters how much money they had to collect from them. The system changed the power dynamics of the restaurant; while earlier the control had been with the waiters, it was now with us.

The change ensured that we got all the money we were earning and our sale collections started to shoot up. We removed the system of the central jar and let them keep the tips they earned in an effort to motivate them, while simultaneously reducing the scope of them cheating their fellow waiters or us.

These changes not only increased our profits substantially, but they also established me as a true leader in the eyes of the people we interacted with. I started to take control over the functioning of Swati and led from the front instead of hiding at the back, and the faith that my family and staff had placed in me started to show its colours.

Soon, Swati, which always had the reputation of a well-established business, started to have the efficiency of one too.

Igniting The Flame

In those days, a majority of the crockery that we used was made of glass and this led to high chances of breakage. Almost every other day, either a customer or a waiter would break a piece of crockery and someone had to rush to clear it up. I would find this quite dangerous. I was afraid that some small pieces of glass would be left behind and could hurt somebody if they accidentally stepped on it, and was not willing to take the responsibility of someone getting injured in the restaurant.

The first thing I did was to change the glass bowls in which ice cream was served into steel bowls. It was the ice cream bowls that would break the most because the condensation on the outside of the bowls would make them slippery and they could easily fall from someone's hand. By switching to steel bowls we eliminated this problem.

However, we couldn't replace all our crockery to steel ones because of the cost and their lack of visual appeal. Instead, I divided the kitchen and created a separate area where the hand-churned ice cream would be made. Previously, I had been worried that some glass pieces from broken crockery would fall into the hand-churner if the staff wasn't careful, and though this never happened, I preferred being extra cautious.

Another food item that was made directly at the small, on-site Swati kitchen was pav bhaji. Besides this and the hand-churned ice cream, the rest of the dishes continued to be made fresh every morning at my mother's home (even

40

after her demise) before being brought to the restaurant. The reason we made pav bhaji at Swati itself was that everyone liked the bhaji in a different way. While some people would not want onions, others wouldn't want potatoes, and yet some others would want both in varying quantities. People also had their own preferences when it came to the level of spice and butter that they wanted in the dish. The bhaji was made on the spot in small quantities so that it could be easily tailored to perfection.

Initially we used to cook on a kitchen stove that took a lot of time. When gas stoves were introduced, we were one of the first restaurants that purchased it. Though it was expensive, I knew that the reduction in time and improved efficiency that it brought about would make the price worth it.

What I didn't realise at the time was that while I was busy igniting the flame on our new gas stove, life had been igniting the flame within me. While I had joined Swati out of compulsion, somehow without me noticing it, I had started to get more involved and engrossed in its daily operations. The changes I made in the two years from 1981 to 1982 didn't go unnoticed and people started to appreciate the touch of professionalism the changes brought while still retaining the homely environment of the place.

Catering To The Crowds

In 1982, my sister-in-law got married and Sailesh and I had gone for one of the functions at a suburban hotel.

While the ceremony progressed beautifully, the food was a big let-down. It was the traditional simple Gujarati spread that people had in those days, but the taste of the food was disappointing. The curd was sour, and the vadas instead of being soft, were very hard. Most of vegetables looked burnt, had wrong proportions of spices and were served with cold, chewy rotis. Even the desserts such as shiro were undercooked and not sweet enough.

On an impulse, I approached my father-in-law and asked him to allow me to do the catering for the main wedding function. I had never done anything like that before, but I was determined to help my sister-in-law, and serve better food at the main wedding function. To my surprise, he agreed, and let a novice like me take over the wedding instead of the professionally appointed caterer. We made an agreement that my father-in-law would pay for the cost of the ingredients and labour, but I would not make any surplus income from it, which was natural since it was a family function.

When I told Viralalji about it, he instantly agreed and we decided to get to work. The wedding was held at Turf Club, at the racecourse at Mahalaxmi in Central Mumbai, and we were allowed to use the Club kitchens for all the cooking. While I was planning the menu, I had only one thought in my mind: I wanted the food to be unique.

In those days, only simple Gujarati meals were served at Gujarati weddings, with the same dishes made in the same manner each time. I wanted to add my own twist to the dishes so that the guests had something unique to remember the wedding by.

For starters we had *khaman dhokla* and *dahi vadas* served in a *matti ka kullad,* which made them look very attractive. For the main course, we had the seasonal vegetable of undhiya with bhindi ki sabzi, and moong dal that could be eaten with fried puris or rice. Instead of serving rice in bowls, we wrapped up the rice in banana leaves and then steamed them to create rice-in-blankets that the guests could then unwrap and eat. We also engaged the services of more cooks so that the puris were hot and fresh when they reached the guests. For desserts we had delicious jalebis fresh off the *kadai,* and warm, sweet shiro garnished with chopped almonds.

In this manner, Viralalji and I designed the entire 12-dish menu that would be served to around 1,200 guests for lunch, and another 15-dish menu that would be served to 2,000 people at dinner, covering both meals at the day-long wedding function. To say that I had never undertaken an endeavour of this magnitude was putting it mildly, and I was nervous and excited at the same time.

The food was a big hit. It was the first time that most of the guests had eaten food that reminded them of home, and yet had an exotic flavour to it. The guests were generous with their praises and soon the entire wedding party was abuzz with the talk of the new caterer in town – Swati Snacks.

I had done this wedding out of love for my sister-in-law and never expected it to go so well. But before I knew it, we were getting booked for wedding catering orders by most of the guests who had upcoming weddings in their own families and thus we embarked on a new journey.

7

Expanding My Boundaries

DURING THE YEARS 1982 TO 1985 THERE WERE MANY stumbling blocks that I had to overcome. Situations kept arising, one after another, testing my endurance and pushing me to expand my boundaries. A lot of the situations I faced brought forth childhood fears and insecurities and I knew it was time to face them head on.

My childhood home in Gowalia Tank was in the same lane as the local police station and we got to see the police in action very often. My friends and I would often play a game called 'chor police'. All the children would be divided into two groups – one team would be robbers and the other would be the police. The aim of the game was for the robbers to run and hide while the police tried to catch them. It was a harmless game, commonly played by children in those days. But one day, it became all too real for me.

In 1954, when I was nine-years-old, I was standing outside my building when I heard a lot of commotion on

44

the road. I turned to see a man running while the police chased him. Suddenly one policeman dived, landing on the man (presumably a robber), and pushed him to the ground. The other policemen quickly surrounded the robber and handcuffed him. The robber was then unceremoniously dragged on the ground up to the police station as he begged for mercy.

While the nearby pedestrians applauded the bravery of the policemen, I was too young and scared to realise that they had carried out a valiant act. All I remember thinking was that the police were big, scary men who would lock me up in jail if I did anything wrong.

This fear of the police got lodged in my heart at a very young age, and even as an adult I found it very difficult to shake it off.

After I joined Swati in 1979, I frequently had to deal with the police. But instead of being able to talk to them calmly, I would want to run away from them, scared that I would do or say something wrong and then get into trouble for it.

A frequent cause of my run-ins with the police was that the lane outside Swati would get filled up with cars. People would double-park their cars outside the restaurant and come inside to eat, which was the only option at the time as not many people could afford drivers. The police didn't appreciate customers blocking the road and would spare no opportunity to remind me of the same.

The sight of these big, bulky men dressed in uniform storming into Swati, would send chills down my spine and my voice would tremble when I would talk to them. They would tell me that I had to have the cars removed immediately or they would fine everyone and tow away the cars. I never had the courage to stand up and ask them what exactly they wanted me to do to solve this problem once and for all, and I would just keep apologising until they went away. I wanted them to leave Swati as fast as possible because I knew that the frequent visits of the police would not be good for business or for Swati's reputation.

When the police would stride in and demand that the cars be moved immediately, I had no choice but to request the customers to do so and they would get angry with me. The customers would remark that they had come to Swati to enjoy a meal and not to get caught or penalised by the police. They would get very upset when I would ask them to move their cars and many of them even took to yelling at me in front of my staff and other customers. Some customers would scream and say that I was incompetent and had no idea how to run a business, and did whatever they could to make sure that I was embarrassed and humiliated in my own restaurant. They were overdramatic and easily offended, but I wasn't brave enough to call them out on this.

I was always fearful of people who showed their temper and their words brought forth my own insecurities. The feelings I had in my school days about not being good enough came flooding back and I would believe them when they said that I didn't know what I was doing.

I would keep apologising to them and try getting them to settle down.

Those days, caught between the police yelling at me on one hand and the customers screaming on the other, I would feel so uncomfortable and upset that I just wanted to run away. I would tell my staff while I left in the evening that no matter what, I would not come back the next day.

There were many customers who seemed to be on the lookout for an opportunity to throw a fit. Once they had placed their order, they would always be alert to make sure that their order came first. Besides, they would also keep tabs on when and what nearby tables were ordering. If by chance, an order that was placed after theirs was served before theirs, all hell broke loose.

They would stand up and start accusing the waiters of partiality and when that did not satisfy them, they would march up to the cash counter and take out their residual anger on me. It didn't matter if the cooking times for different orders differed, or if one dish required less time assembling than the other. All that mattered in their eyes was that they had been cheated out of their 'right' to be served first and they spared no opportunity to inform us of that.

I used to be scared that if a customer left unhappy, they would not come back and Swati would eventually lose all its customers. I was always under the assumption that if I made a mistake or said something wrong, I would lose the business my mother had worked so hard to build. In this situation, my self-esteem and self-respect took a backseat, and I let everyone walk over me as long as it meant that they would leave Swati happy.

It took me a long time to realise the difference between loyal customers and big bullies. While the former came for the taste of the food and gave back in love, the latter took away the love and left a bad taste behind.

8

Raising Boys With Freedom

WHEN I GOT MARRIED AND EVENTUALLY JOINED SWATI, Anand had settled down in Ahmedabad. He had first gone there to study architecture, and was raising a family of his own. He had two boys, Shaan and Neel, who were born in 1973 and 1976 respectively. As little boys, they were a delightful combination of Anand and his wife Shyama, and I loved spending as much time as I could with them. Though Anand and Shyama had never formally married because they didn't believe in the concept of a legally binding marriage, they were life partners in the truest sense of the term, and still are, to this day.

The only thing that came between Anand and I was distance, though we tried our best not to let it affect us. When our mother was there, she went almost once a month to visit them from Mumbai but being married myself, I could not manage to go more than once in two or three months because of my responsibilities at home.

49

To compensate for this, Anand and his family would come and live with us whenever they could.

Anand and I made all our plans keeping his boys in mind so that they could grow up surrounded by the people who loved them. There wasn't a single moment where it felt that Anand and I had separate families and we were as close as one happy, joint family spread across two cities.

I didn't have children of my own and this made my relationship with the boys even deeper. I never felt that they were Anand's children and that I was just their *bua*; it felt as if they were my children too.

Though the times had changed since we were young, and people were getting more protective as well as pressurising of their children, Anand stuck to his values and raised his boys the way we had been brought up.

In 1979, when I took over Swati, Anand made it a point to get the boys to the restaurant as often as he could. The boys would run around and play with the staff who in turn would treat the boys as little princes who had returned to their kingdom. Their joyful energy and pure love infused the restaurant with the much-needed vibrancy that had fallen flat after my mother's passing.

Armed with a camera, the boys would shoot many videos of Viralalji cooking, as he patiently explained the different ingredients and methods over and over again. The boys would never tire of listening to his stories and would keep asking him to repeat his words, capturing the talks from different angles every time. Viralalji, who had raised Anand and me when we were young, was more than delighted to repeat his nurturing with Anand's boys now.

At home, the boys would try and imitate Viralalji's cooking with their plastic kitchen set and serve me empty plates, imagined to be filled with pani puri, pav bhaji, or whatever dish they had learnt about that day. I was only too proud to sample this imaginary food and declare it as the best food I had eaten in my life. In many ways, the love that they served me along with the empty plates made the declaration ring true.

Shaan and Neel grew up with warmth and joy as their constant companions, and every day they would meet new people in Swati who couldn't help but fall in love with them the way we had.

In 1985, Anand, Shyama, the boys, and I, took a week's trip to Gulmarg, Pehelgaum, and Srinagar – popular winter destinations in India's northernmost state (now union territory) of Kashmir.

When we went to Gulmarg, we spent a lot of time playing in the snow and taking miniature golf lessons. It was the first time any of us had tried that sport, and after a lot of embarrassing mistakes, we finally got the hang of it. We put this newfound knowledge of golf to use when we reached Srinagar and saw that our hotel had its own golf course. The boys and I would happily play together for hours, giving Anand and Shyama a well-deserved break together.

We visited various tourist attractions, sampling local cuisine, and collecting souvenirs. The week passed all too soon and we came back with our suitcases heavy and hearts full.

Preparation For Life

Back at home, Shaan and Neel hated the restrictions in school and the pressure to perform. They had inherited my aversion to school and would always want to run away from there. In 1986, when Shaan was in Class 6 – at the same age I was when I failed in school – he became very fearful of his upcoming exams. He would cry continuously for many nights, terrified of going back to school. He became quiet and withdrawn, and would only open his mouth to beg his parents to let him stay at home.

Anand had seen this behaviour with me, and knew the lasting impact it had on my life because I had been forced to go to an institution that made me feel unworthy every day. I had grown up with a deep sense of inadequacy and fear of authorities that lasted well into my adult life and impacted everything I did. He knew that no matter what, he didn't want the same emotions to rankle his boys. He spoke to Shyama about this, and within a few days, they pulled both their boys out of school.

People were shocked at their decision, and till today, when they hear about it, they find it hard to believe. Many people told him that he was ruining his boys' lives by not forcing them to complete their education. But Anand and Shyama were firm in their belief. They knew that both their boys were equipped with the basic foundation of education, and that whatever additional skills they needed would be provided by life itself.

The boys grew up in the best manner possible; the way all children had grown up before institutionalised schooling took their childhoods away. They spent their time climbing trees in Anand's large farmhouse, playing all kinds of sports, and reading the books that piqued their curiosity. Their growth was nurtured by their parents and tended to by life itself.

Life, instead of being a struggle, was an adventure for them. Their world didn't revolve around competitions and exams; it revolved around the changing seasons and the hugely friendly intelligence of life that guided them through it.

9

Knives Out

ONCE I TOOK OVER SWATI, WITHIN A FEW YEARS, THE STAFF was split into two clear sides. On one side was the older staff, the ones whose loyalty my mother had nurtured and won over the decades. They had an impeccable work ethic and a strong conscience. On the other side were the newer staff members. They were the ones who had come to make quick money and would work carelessly, hurriedly rushing from one job to another. This difference was easily noticeable to anyone who entered the kitchen, and the two sides had a difficult time trying to understand or relate to the other's point of view.

Though by 1985 only a few of our senior staff like Devji and Viralalji remained, they ran a tight ship and would not hesitate to out anyone who tried to skimp on their duties. The newer staff didn't like being called out and revolted against it. They felt that Viralalji should take their side and support them since they were from the same village and social strata. For the senior staff, however, I was as much a daughter to them as their own daughters back home, and they were caught in the hard place of wanting to protect the restaurant and not wanting to punish their fellow workers.

Every few weeks a fight would break out between the two parties and I would be stuck as the mediator. I was always scared of being short-staffed and gave into the demands of the new staff more than I should have, just to get them to stay. The newer staff knew of this fear and would take any opportunity to exploit it.

If Viralalji ever screamed at them for something, they would come to me and threaten to quit in large numbers if I didn't get Viralalji to back down. These threats to quit were frequent and worked almost every time because I didn't think I would be able to keep the restaurant running without adequate staff.

These ultimatums were especially popular during Diwali time when I would give them their yearly bonus and increase their salary proportionately to the work they had done. The method of proportional increase, instead of a standard one, was fair and had been in place since decades, but with the new staff it didn't work any longer. They would talk amongst themselves about how much bonus they were getting and what their salary increment was, and armed with that information they would come to me and fight.

They would accuse me of partiality and demand explanations for how some of the staff was getting more money. They would say they were quitting because they didn't want to work in a place that treated the staff so unfairly. I used to think that if they did so, not only would I lose waiters, but it would also harm the reputation of the restaurant in all working circles. Afraid of these outcomes, I would accept their demands and raise their salaries equally.

Before Swati, I had never worked at any place or handled a business; I hadn't ever planned to. When a sudden turn of events threw me into the spotlight, I had no one to guide me through it or teach me the ropes. That time my only aim was to keep the business running and not to let Swati – that my mother had so lovingly built – lose its reputation. I fell into a trap of allowing people to walk over me for what I considered to be the greater good – having Swati continue operating at any cost.

During the initial six or seven years, from 1979 to 1985, I faced many obstacles from customers, and the staff. In many cases I would work out profitable solutions that could satisfy both parties, but if I found the other party getting aggressive I would quickly back down. They would yell at me and I would apologise for whatever inconvenience I may have caused them.

Matters finally came to a head one day when some of the staff members showed up, inebriated, for work. Viralalji noticed this as soon as they entered and quickly got rid of them from the back door. He fired them on the spot and warned them not to be seen around Swati in the future. I thought the matter would end there and didn't think more about it.

The next day, the men who had been fired, came back and asked to speak to Viralalji outside. I wasn't in the kitchen at that time to decline this and Viralalji went with them. It seemed that the men were part of a local street gang, and they rounded up Viralalji and started pushing him around, bullying him for having the audacity to fire them. When I heard the commotion and looked out of the window, matters had escalated quickly and I couldn't believe what I was seeing – one of the men held a knife to Viralalji's throat and was threatening to kill him.

I rushed out of the shop and I think the men were as surprised to see me as I had been to see them, and they paused, not sure what to do. I took the opportunity their hesitation provided me and told them that I would call the police to throw them all in jail if they didn't leave that instant and promised never to return. There must have been something in my voice or my stance, some unknown power they hadn't seen before, which made them realise beyond doubt that I would act on my words.

Later that night, when I was thinking about the incident, the irony of the situation didn't escape me. I hadn't hesitated for a moment to confront my former staff who were local gang members, but I was scared to talk to my customers and team on a daily basis. That day, for the first time, I got a glimpse of the reservoir of power that existed within me, and that frankly exists within each one of us, just waiting for a chance to express itself.

I realised that though sometimes I feel weak or inadequate, the same universal force that ran through the strongest people in the world, also ran through me. That incident could have gone either way, but it went in our favour, convincing me that in life we are only given as much as we can handle.

As this realisation started to take shape in me, I went from feeling invisible to knowing that I could stand up to the bullies in my life.

The Wisdom Of Life

Looking back, I can see how many obstacles I had to deal with, but at that time it didn't feel that way. While I was going through those situations, I didn't view them as problems. I just thought that they were part of the job and I had to deal with them. Since I hadn't done anything like running a restaurant before, I didn't have anything to compare my experience with and judge it as 'good' or 'bad'.

I didn't have any goals of making a lot of money or making Swati more famous. I simply did what I could and dealt with situations to the best of my ability. I believe that it was this lack of expectations, or desire for particular outcomes, that helped me to steer the boat of Swati to calmer waters and not get lost under the high waves. It was due to this that I remained happy and peaceful despite the challenges at work in the initial years.

There were many people who helped me to keep going with their kind words of support when I was feeling low. Help poured in from all sides, encouraging me to continue, just when I was about to give up.

My nani came to Swati once a month to eat the hand-churned ice cream. She would sit with me and talk for hours, and her presence was as much of a comfort for me as it had been during my school days.

Older customers who had known and loved my mother would always spare a few moments at the end of their meal to remind me that my mother would have been proud of me if she could have seen me then – running Swati the same way she had and not letting the standards fall.

The restaurant was always packed with loyal customers and catered to people from many strata of society. Besides the initial investment that my nani had given of Rs.35,000, Swati ran on its own money and we never had to borrow from others or compromise on our savings. This helped us pay for quality ingredients as well as the efficient staff.

Generations of families, including old couples with their grandchildren, uncles, aunts and younger cousins would come and dine together, marvelling at the flavour of the food that had remained unchanged for decades. Popular items included dahi puri, sugarcane juice and sitaphal ice cream. The older staff at Swati kept up this consistency in the taste by meticulously creating the same recipes day after day and passing down these skills to the juniors. They never took shortcuts in their work and in fact did more than they were asked to in order to help us pull through the rough patches.

Owners of other restaurants like the proprietor of the Shiv Sagar eatery, who knew my husband, put aside competitive differences and came forward to help and guide me through the technical aspects of running a restaurant. It was from them that I learnt to judge when I was being cheated and when I was getting a good deal from the various vendors we interacted with.

Most of all, my brother Anand reached out to me by phone every day, and would come to Mumbai as often as he could, just to make sure that I was all right and that I was happy.

Though, to an outsider, it appeared that Swati rose in popularity solely because of my effort, it was actually an outcome of the efforts of countless people, whether directly in the case of the staff or indirectly in the form of blessings of the customers.

Over the years, just as I helped Swati, Swati also helped me grow. The more time I spent at the restaurant, experimenting with flavours, training staff, and learning from new challenges, the more confidence I got in my abilities and in my potential. It was through Swati that I learnt to believe in the wisdom of life and in the magic of possibilities.

Faith – My Anchor

One of the reasons why I could hold on to my inner state of happiness and peace, despite the challenging situations outside, was due to the foundation of yoga and prayer that I had built up over decades.

My faith in a Higher Power helped me gain faith in myself and in the mechanisms of the world, which were bringing me to each stage of my life. Everyone needs something they can rely on when times get tough, be it a person, a place, or an inner state of being. For me, it was the Divine – though It came to me in many different forms.

As a young girl, I had accompanied my nani to the local Jain temple and learnt various shlokas and stories about our religion. My favourite shloka was the Navkar Mantra and I chanted it every day for many years. This helped the mantra get internalised and I could use it as a shield to protect myself from the outside world when things got difficult. This practice continued even I after I got married, and the ritual of sitting and praying with my new family helped us to bond and build connections with each other.

In 1977, when I was 32 years old, I started learning yoga from the Kaivalyadham School of Yoga in Mumbai. A teacher from the institution would come home every day and guide me through the different yoga *asanas*. Over the course of a few months, my body started to gain flexibility and agility, and I could train my body to be still along with my mind. The peace that I had been feeling in my mind with the shlokas now started to penetrate my body with the help of the asanas.

When my mother passed away in 1979, I felt completely lost and my belief in Jainism started to decline. At that time, Viralalji used to be a big devotee of Lord Ram and introduced me to his form of worship. I took to it immediately and started to dedicate a lot of my time to it. Soon, I purchased a copy of the *Ramcharitmanas* and would read it as frequently as I could.

Over time, when I would go to my mother's home

(where now only Viralalji and Devji lived, and the food of Swati would get cooked), I would carry the Ramcharitmanas with me and read it aloud for the benefit of whoever was present. Viralalji, Devji and other staff members would sit around me in a circle as I read from this book to them.

These moments of sitting on the floor with my staff as equals, bowing down to a Higher Power, brought a new richness to our otherwise mundane boss and employee relationship.

Around 1986, I had started to have a lot of pain in my back for which I could find no adequate medical cure. My friend recommended her yoga teacher to me who had healed her of a lot of similar pains and ailments. On her advice, I switched over to her teacher and then started learning yoga under the Iyengar School of thought. The custom of a teacher coming home every day continued, and my yoga practice grew and flourished under his watchful eye. My pain soon subsided and was replaced by a feeling of strength and power.

My yoga teacher was an ardent follower of Lord Shiva, and while taking the class, he would talk a lot about his faith. I was keen to hear his stories and always asked him to tell me more. He encouraged me to try learning about Lord Shiva on my own and asked me to go to a temple at Mahalaxmi (a fifteen-minute drive from my home) for their daily Shiva puja.

The more I learnt about Lord Shiva, the more I started to connect with Him. I frequented the Mahalaxmi temple so often that I got to know the priests and the temple staff, and would stay behind after the puja to talk to them. They would also serve delicious *prasad* after the *aarti* such as *yellow peda* and *white mava peda*. Over time, I established a small temple dedicated to Lord Shiva in my own home, and would start and end my day by sitting in front of Him. I also started performing *Rudra puja* once a year at my home that everyone could attend. This practice continued for many years and helped me through many situations in my life.

As I evolved as a person, the form of the Divine also evolved with me. But while the appearance kept changing, the essence never did; and my faith became the anchor that kept me steady amidst the swirling waters of mind and life.

10

Home For All

THE MONEY WE GOT FROM CATERING WAS VERY LUCRATIVE and helped us popularise Swati further.

Initially, all the orders for catering that we received were from our own Jain-Gujarati community, most of whom had attended my sister-in-law's wedding or knew someone who had gone and loved the food. We would take up catering orders only once in six months because the rest of the time needed to be devoted to Swati and keeping it running on a daily basis.

The first order we received from outside our community was for the daughter of the owner of Fiat Cars – the most popular car in those days. The wedding was in 1990, and was held at the distinguished Turf Club. The wedding was between two people from the Maharashtrian and Gujarati communities and the food was Gujarati cuisine with a twist, which had become our signature style. For starters we had *til dhoklas* and *skin potatoes*. In the main course, we had the seasonal undhiya vegetable accompanied with coconut rice (served in a coconut shell), and *pakoda kadhi*. For dessert, we served *orange basundi* and *churma ladoo*. The food was widely appreciated by people from both communities and we soon managed to expand our catering customer base to people from different communities across Mumbai.

My mother had inculcated in me the idea that a business could truly rise only when its workers were rising with it. No place could be successful if the people helping it to grow remained unsuccessful and unfulfilled in their own personal lives.

As the money started to come in, I started keeping parts of it aside for a staff fund. When we had collected enough, I purchased a small space in the nearby *chawl* and gave it to my staff for them to live in. A lot of them were either from the suburbs or from out of Mumbai and having their own space to come back to at the end of a long day was a boon for them.

Previously, many of them had to travel long hours to reach work or would stay with relatives or in shanties nearby, hopping from one place to another, with nowhere to settle down in the harsh summers or long monsoons. This space was like their home away from home, and helped them look at Swati as family and not just another job. With this, I managed to win their loyalty and gratitude for life, similar to what my mother had during her time.

Open For Lunch

Up until the late 1990s, Swati had been open from 3 to 10 p.m., serving only evening snacks and dinner. But around 1998, I started to feel that we were not using our resources adequately and that much could be done if we extended the working hours of the restaurant. After speaking to Viralalji, we decided that Swati would now be open from noon to 10 p.m. Though Devji had retired earlier the same year, he had recruited and trained two more cooks who took up the work after him and looking at their drive and commitment, I knew that they would also be able to handle the additional responsibilities.

The biggest challenge in terms of the new initiative was that of creating a lunch menu because people would not prefer to eat chaat during that time, since chaat was primarily considered to be an evening snack or light meal for dinner.

When we were children, our mother had exposed us to many different cuisines and even unusual recipes within our traditional cuisine that proved very useful for me as we planned the lunch menu. I decided to introduce some recipes from my childhood, with a few variations to see whether our customers liked them.

The first dish was *panki*. Back in the day, very few people in Mumbai had heard about panki and even fewer had tasted it. We had loved the dish while growing up and knew the customers would too – if only they would order it. During the initial years of introducing it, only three or four pankis would get sold in a day and it took many years and a lot of word-of-mouth marketing for those numbers to rise. I'm glad that we stuck with our instincts and didn't pull it off the menu because today, almost 300-400 pankis get sold every single day.

Malpua was a dish I had first sampled at a Rajashthani fair and immediately loved it. But instead of presenting it the traditional way, I wanted to add my own Gujarati spin on it. Usually, malpua is a single-layer pancake that is deep fried. We stuffed the malpua with *malai,* rolled it and then put *chashni* on top of it. The malai added the richness to the malpua because the flavour was enhanced due to the stuffing. This variation made the dish stand out and the customers immediately took to it. Initially we sold around five malpuas a day, and now we sell six times as much, with 30 malpuas being sold in a day.

We even invented a few recipes from scratch, such as the *satpadi roti.* We knew we couldn't serve the roti plain and introduced *gatte ka saag* to go with it, and soon it became a lunch favourite. When it was introduced, we would serve only ten plates a day, but now more than 70 plates are ordered each day.

Another item we introduced was *fada ni khichree,* a staple in many Gujarati households that we knew would be popular with our traditional crowd. It has steadily risen in popularity even with the non-Gujarati crowd, with 75 plates being sold every day, up from the initial ten.

These new additions were a hit and it wasn't long before the place was packed with customers on weekdays, and we had long lines forming outside the restaurant on most weekends.

Grounded Through Fame

Though all our customers were equally valuable to us, there were a few names that stood out and helped take Swati's name to the elite social circles of Mumbai. One of our Sunday regulars was M.F. Husain, the famous painter; his favourite dish was sev puri, and his artistic tendencies were evident to all in the way he always came barefoot to the restaurant. Other notable guests included the Ambani family, Zakir Hussain (an Indian musician maestro), television artists, and many cricketers. Not only did they come to Swati to eat, but we also went to their homes when invited for catering functions. One of our first outstation catering orders in Calcutta, West Bengal, was for Mr. and Mrs. Goenka, a popular industrialist family in those days.

In 1999, Rashmi Uday Singh, a popular food critic from *The Times of India* newspaper came to Swati to try the food and to interview me. Her glowing review of the restaurant was one of the highlights of the year and helped spread the name of Swati even further.

I started getting requests from all corners of India and the world, including New York, London, Dubai, and Singapore, for starting franchises. Everyone wanted a part of Swati and they were willing to pay handsomely for it. But Swati wasn't just a business for me, it had been my mother's baby, and was as much a part of the family as any of us were. My mother was never keen on selling it or giving control to others and I wasn't either.

Besides, I knew how much effort it took to maintain

the taste and quality of the food. It was very easy to want to start something, but maintaining the standard, much less raising it, was a task very few were capable of. If I franchised Swati, and the people could not maintain the perfection of the food, the reputation of the restaurant would suffer and impact every branch of Swati including the original one that we had spent decades building.

These offers were tempting, but I knew I had to stand my ground for the greater good of the restaurant. I realised that one has to make tough decisions not only in times of trouble but also in times of prosperity. Keeping my feet firmly planted on the ground prevented us from being swept away by the tides of fortune and misfortune.

11

A Cause For Celebration

IN THE MEANTIME, LIFE AT HOME HAD BEEN PROGRESSING smoothly. Sailesh and I had two favourite restaurants in the city where we would go to eat on the days I didn't have to be at Swati. One of them was Paradise restaurant at Colaba – a popular tourist locality in South Mumbai. It was famous for its non-vegetarian food but, being vegetarian, we loved to have the white bread chutney sandwiches (they were famous for the softness of their breads and sweet green chutney), and cold coffee with vanilla ice cream. Another favourite hangout for us was Satkar restaurant at Churchgate (a business as well as residential area near the sea) and we went there often, to eat South Indian food. Our favourite dishes were the sada dosas and idlis served with piping hot sambhar and chutney.

I was also a member of the Willingdon Sports Club located near my house at Tardeo. I decided to start taking golf lessons at the Club while Sailesh was at work, and found myself a coach to help teach me the art of the sport. Sailesh had gifted me a car and I would drive it to the Club, learn golf, and then drive myself to Swati by afternoon to manage the affairs there. Golf was a very enjoyable sport and though I never played competitively, it gave me a great deal of skill and finesse that I utilised in other aspects of my life.

Anand's boys were growing up and as they had lesser time to come to Mumbai, I used to take Mumbai to them. Once every few months, I would pack the ingredients needed to make their favourite dishes of pani puri and bhel from Swati and fly with it to Ahmedabad. The boys liked their pani puri slightly spicy and so I would make it for them without meethi chutney. They could easily eat at least 15-20 puris in one sitting each, accompanied with a generous helping of bhel on the side. They were growing boys with big appetites, and watching them eat with so much enthusiasm was one of the delights of my trip. The boys knew I would always come bearing treats and their eyes would light up when they saw me enter their house accompanied with bags of ingredients.

In 1992, Anand's family and I went for a holiday to Disneyland, Orlando. Shaan and Neel were 22 and 19 years respectively and loved going on roller coasters. We were there for almost a week and we spent practically every day at Disneyland.

We went for every roller coaster ride there was, the scarier the better. We loved the thrill of our cart slowly climbing up the tracks, the moment of anticipation right before the big drop, and the rush of adrenaline when the cart started zooming towards the ground. We would scream and shout with laughter as our hearts raced in our chests, our hands thrown up to the sky, unafraid as we swooped down, went upside down in circles, and swished from one side of the cart to the other.

Shyama and Anand happily watched from below, taking pictures as we came back from the rides with our cheeks red from exhilaration. We ate a lot of Mexican food on that trip, especially *tacos, enchiladas,* and a wide variety of desserts such as chocolate ice cream and *churros.* It was an unforgettable trip and one of the last big family vacations that we took.

The lack of formal schooling never impacted the boys or hindered their growth in any way. By the time they reached adulthood, they were equipped with the greatest skills of all – they knew how to be brave and kind and loving. They had faith in life and in the joyful purity of innocence. They not only succeeded in life, they excelled in it.

Shaan and Neel took the field of construction and architecture by storm with the company they started with Anand, and their name is associated with prestige and quality across Ahmedabad till today.

In 1998, Shaan married a wonderful girl named Maushami, and in 1999, Neel met Sheryl and they soon started families of their own.

Shaan had two children, elder daughter Niva and son Akash, and Neel had a daughter named Ria. The two families continued to live in Anand's farmhouse where they had been raised, but they built two separate bungalows in the same compound to have both, the privacy of nuclear families and the companionship of joint families.

The younger generation, my grandchildren, were my pride and joy. They were much calmer than their mischievous fathers but alike them in so many ways. I used to sit in the room playing 'kitchen set' with them for hours on end, much like I had done with Shaan and Neel, and I used to take them on tours of Swati every time they came to Mumbai to visit. I would introduce them to everyone as the 'future owners' of Swati and they were so adorable that neither the staff nor the customers could resist playing with them. I used to jokingly tell Shaan and Neel that their babies were the best gift they could have ever given me; and in many ways that was true.

12

Ready, Set, Hire!

BY THE YEAR 2000, WE HAD ENOUGH MONEY SAVED UP, both from the daily running of the restaurant and the catering business, so that we could look at expanding the restaurant. We purchased the radio shop adjoining Swati and started integrating it with the existing space so that it could now seat 85 people – more than double its previous capacity of 40 people.

Our architect, Rahul Mehrotra, designed the space with many inputs from Anand, especially when it came to choosing the furniture that he sent across from Ahmedabad. I didn't interfere much with the design or layout and was happy to leave it in the capable hands of my brother. However, all aspects of how the restaurant would be actually run was completely in my hands and along with Viralalji, I came up with a plan to use the additional space effectively and effortlessly.

One of the setbacks we encountered was when it came to the hiring and training of the staff. While the task might seem easy, not all employees are equally talented, and they can't perform beyond their capacity. Generally, and even at Swati, the staff was divided into three categories. The first comprised of cooks, second of waiters, and the third of water boys. Everyone at Swati was required to start as a water boy and then work themselves up to positions of authority.

Water boys would serve you water and clear up your plates when you were finished with your food. Once they had learnt how to hold large trays, how to serve customers water and how to keep an eye out to refill the glasses as soon as they were empty, they were then moved up to the position of waiter.

Waiters would be responsible for taking orders, addressing questions, and making sure the correct orders were delivered as per the specifications, to each table. One of the toughest parts for the water boys was becoming familiar with the dishes. Since the food at Swati was so unique, most of them hadn't eaten or even heard about those dishes before. Being water boys gave them a chance to become accustomed to the food but they still needed personal training to memorise the vast menu.

Another important part of the waiter's job was to answer customer queries. The most common question was, 'What is this made out of?' But the background to this question was deeper than it seemed. Many times, other chefs or restaurant owners would come to Swati in the hope of stealing and imitating our recipes. So the seemingly harmless question of 'What is this made of?' could hide a desire to poach the recipe behind it. Waiters had to be vigilant enough to decide whether this was a genuine, innocent customer query or an underhand tactic. New waiters were not allowed to take this call and had to alert a senior staff member so that they could decide and proceed accordingly.

Cooks were responsible for maintaining the quality of the food and perfectly replicating the dishes that had been prepared for decades. We rarely got trained cooks and most of them were those who had worked their way up from being waiters, and so, had to be taught everything from scratch. We usually got our staff through word-of-mouth advertising and they were all new to this field.

We never hired from hospitality schools or restaurant staff training establishments. Most of the graduates from those schools that we came across were overconfident about their abilities and had no experience of how things actually work in the real world. They were filled with theoretical knowledge, and this was the biggest barrier between them and an open, inquisitive mind that the raw recruits came with.

But training the staff from scratch came with its own share of problems. Many of them would come for work for a few days or a few weeks and then disappear. The badge that they carried, stating 'trained under Swati', would earn them a good 20% higher salary than the market rate, and there was no shortage of people wanting to poach staff from Swati. This couldn't be helped in most cases of water boys and waiters as there was no way to know who would stay and who would leave. But this was why being a cook at Swati was very difficult. It required years of loyalty and work, first as a water boy, then as a waiter, before they were allowed to come anywhere in contact with our recipes or cooking methods.

Another issue that frequently came up when we first expanded was fighting amongst the staff. The large number of people we hired shook up the environment of the place initially, and it took a few weeks for everyone to settle into their new roles and relationships with each other. Usually, the fights were just small verbal altercations; issues would crop up for a few moments and settle down on their own. It was nothing serious, and nothing for me to concern myself with.

One day, however, two members of the staff got into a heated argument with each other, and despite intervention by other staff members, they refused to back down. The tension increased to such a level that they started picking up utensils and hitting each other with them. The senior staff members jumped in the middle, grabbled them both, and removed them from the back door of the restaurant. Later on, when I came to know about it, I immediately fired them; a hot temper was always bad news in the kitchen because you are around food and many breakable items. Safety of the staff, food, and customers was always my top priority as a restaurateur.

During the same year, I also purchased a small space in the same lane as Swati that could be used as our kitchen. Up until then, all food had been cooked in my mother's home every morning before being brought to the restaurant. Swati itself only had a basic pantry and couldn't accommodate a full-fledged kitchen, so having a kitchen in the same lane was the next best option.

By around 7 a.m. every morning the staff would reach the kitchen and start preparing food and by 11 a.m. they would carry it on their cycles to the restaurant that was to open at noon.

It had been 21 years since I first joined Swati and I was now actively involved in every aspect of the restaurant. I would drop by Swati twice a day, once in the morning to ensure that all preparations were going smoothly, and once in the evening to check on the day's sales and accounts.

A matter that I noticed was that since our staff kept increasing, they were finding it difficult to find space for themselves when it was time for them to eat their own lunch or take a break. The pantry we had inside Swati was always overflowing with vessels, staff, and food, and there was hardly a place to stand comfortably.

In 2004, now with more resources in hand, I purchased a one-bedroom flat in the same building as Swati. One room was turned into a staff room where there were benches and chairs for the staff to eat comfortably and for rest breaks. The kitchen was made into a cleaning room where soiled utensils were kept and cleaned before being returned to the restaurant, and the hall was made into an office, where I hired an accountant to sit each day and keep track of the money and accounts. This expansion freed up a lot of space in Swati and made the restaurant look bigger and neater too.

As and when we could afford it, I kept up with my

practice of buying rooms in chawls for the staff so that they could have a place to stay and go back to after working at Swati. A few of the staff members had to share the room in each chawl that not only encouraged bonding between them but also made them value Swati, because they knew that if they left or were removed, they would lose their place to stay too.

13

Swati Must Stay In The Family

BY 2003, SWATI HAD BEEN RUNNING SUCCESSFULLY AND independently for many years. Our staff had settled in after expansion, we had regular customers and were being recognised and awarded for our work. All in all, life at Swati was good and progressing smoothly. However, I always had a niggling fear at the back of my mind, and knew that I finally had to address it.

In 2003, I turned 58 years old and started to get worried about who would look after Swati once I passed away. I didn't have any children to pass it on to, and yet, like my mother I knew that I wanted Swati to remain in the family. My mother had passed away in her 50s and I wanted to have a concrete plan in place so that even if something adverse were to happen to me, the future of Swati would be secured and the burden of looking after it wouldn't suddenly fall on someone else's shoulders the way it had fallen on mine.

The only family I could think of was Anand and his

children in Ahmedabad. They already had their own architecture business but I knew we would have to find a way to make it work if we wanted Swati to be in the family. The next time I went to visit them, I proposed my plan; I suggested that we should open a branch of Swati in Ahmedabad. Since Ahmedabad was a hub of the Gujarati-Jain community, our food would surely sell well there. More than that, Anand and his children would have a chance to understand how the restaurant was run since they would be the ones primarily handling it. I would also be there whenever I could, especially in the initial stages, to help them set everything up and teach them the ropes.

I thought this was a simple yet wonderful plan, because they were getting a chance to learn about the restaurant without leaving their current professions and I would be there to guide them each step of the way. I thought it would be an easier learning curve for them, and once they knew how to handle the Swati restaurant in Ahmedabad, they would be able to handle the Mumbai Swati too, after my demise. But Anand flatly refused.

Suddenly the roles switched; Anand gave all the excuses and reasons that I had initially given when I was forced to join, and I became the cheerleader telling him that everything would be fine. Anand would say that he didn't have any experience in running a restaurant, and I would reason that if I had managed to learn, he would too. When Shaan and Neel would argue that they were just not interested, I would put my foot down and say that Swati had to stay in the family. If they didn't want to do it themselves, they had to find another way to make it work. These discussions continued for almost a year with neither side willing to back down.

Ultimately, however, they knew that the best decision was for Swati to stay in the family because that is what my mother would have wanted. So Shaan and Neel bravely decided to try it out and Anand, of course, jumped on board soon after, and the idea gradually began to take shape.

Ahmedabad, Here We Come!

The first thing we had to do was look for a space. Luckily, Anand was able to purchase land at one of the most sought-after localities called Law Garden. The area was popular among locals and tourists alike because of the roadside vendors who would sell chaat over there. Anand and his boys started constructing a three-storey building: while the ground floor became the seating area of Swati, the first floor became the kitchen, and the second and third floors were made into a furniture store that had always been Anand's dream as an architect.

Since the locality was already famous for chaat, we knew that it would attract the right type of crowd. Moreover, our experience had shown us that given a choice, most people would prefer a slightly more expensive but considerably safer option of eating chaat in a restaurant as compared with a roadside vendor. The restaurant was a half-hour drive away from Anand's farmhouse on busy days, which meant that it would be easy for them to commute from their home to Swati. The restaurant itself was spacious, elegant and could seat up to 80 people.

While Anand and his boys set about constructing the building, I started to work at the restaurant aspects such as hiring people and selecting vendors for vegetables and grains. Selecting chefs was the most important part, and I started to hire them from Mumbai itself since I had more contacts there.

It was a long process, but once we were sure that the people we had hired were smart, hardworking, and loyal, we started to train them to cook our unique recipes. The senior chefs of Swati like Viralalji would take turns to teach the new cooks different recipes and would work with them until they had mastered the dishes.

I was informed once they had completed their training and I decided to test them out. I gave all regular Swati cooks the week off and asked only the new cooks to handle the restaurant. I was sure that if they could handle the Mumbai Swati that was always packed and overflowing with customers, they would easily be able to handle the Ahmedabad Swati.

Much to my delight, they had been trained very well, and there was no test that I could put them through that would be more rigorous than the challenges Viralalji and the other senior cooks had put before them. Once this was settled, I immediately called up Anand and said that things were ready from my end and we could start moving forward.

For the next month, I shifted into Anand's farmhouse in Ahmedabad so that I could focus all my attention on building the new branch of Swati.

One of my main tasks was finding local suppliers to provide us with all the ingredients and produce we would need on a daily basis in the restaurant. I remembered how we had been cheated when I had just started out in Mumbai, but now, after so many years I was a thorough professional. Even in a new city I knew exactly who to ask and where to find the best suppliers for the different items. Negotiations were tricky but once the vendors realised that I already was a well-known restaurateur, they stopped trying to fool me and eagerly jumped on board.

For some reason, however, I could not find a good fruit seller because either their rates were too high or the fruits were not fresh. For the first few months, I would actually courier fruits every week from Mumbai, bearing the additional cost and hassle, just because we didn't want to serve poor quality fruits.

The waiters and water boys had to be hired from Ahmedabad itself since they didn't require much training, but this was a tough job for us. We would try getting them through word-of-mouth advertising like we had done in Mumbai, but in Ahmedabad we were not known among the working circles, so we got all types of workers initially.

In Mumbai we had a reputation for being strict with our staff. Yet, the staff also knew that if they gave us quality work and dedication, they would be rewarded with promotions, a room in the chawls, and access to unlimited opportunities. But this was not the case in Ahmedabad, and we got a lot of waiters who wanted to make quick money without putting in effort. They didn't want to be trained, learn new things or grow as professionals; they just wanted to make money and leave.

Many of the difficulties the waiters had were the same ones we had faced in Mumbai when we had expanded the restaurant to an 85 seater. The waiters found it hard to learn the names of our unique dishes like 'satpadi roti', and even harder to explain to the customers what that dish contained. Another common problem was that they would forget which table had ordered which dish and often end up delivering the wrong item to a table. There was no quick fix to such things. Gradually, as they got accustomed to the seating and numbering arrangement, and the food that we offered, these problems faded away.

We had a soft opening for three days, just to see how the people would respond to our food. A few mistakes were identified and we did our best to rectify or minimise them. Anand and his boys would be out on the floor, making sure that service was going smoothly and interacting with customers to see how they found the experience while I would be in the kitchen making sure that each plate was perfect before we sent it out, and remedying whatever glitches in the assembling or cooking that I found. My daughters-in-law took up the task of coordinating between the chefs in the kitchen and waiters on the floor. Overall, as the three days progressed, we started to get confident that the restaurant would be a success.

Anand soon also efficiently dealt with the problem of hiring loyal staff. He had a large farmhouse where the entire family stayed and where the boys had grown up. They employed a huge staff, from gardeners to housekeepers, and all the children of the staff had grown up playing with Shaan and Neel since they were approximately the same age. They didn't have the notion of belonging to different social classes because Anand had never raised his boys with those views. So when we started facing the problem of disloyal staff, Anand immediately presented the opportunity to work at Swati to all these young men of Shaan's age and they jumped at the offer.

With the influx of these loyal, hardworking men, the entire environment at Swati changed. Since they had grown up looking towards Anand as family, they started to believe that Swati was family, and their baby too; and they started to work towards Swati's success with the same passion and desire as Viralalji and others had, many decades earlier.

I think establishing this branch was easier because we had all our experiences from the Mumbai Swati to fall back on. Many people in the Gujarati-Jain circles had either already tasted our food in Mumbai or had heard rave reviews about it. They came with their friends and family, so even in the initial days we had a steady stream of people coming to try out the food at this branch. The fact that we had managed to replicate the exact taste of the food as in Mumbai and maintained the cosy vibe of the place only added to the whole experience.

As time went on, Anand introduced items unique to the Ahmedabad branch, such as *dal baati* and *patra*. These steadily rose in popularity and now we sell a minimum of 30 plates of both every day.

The reason we didn't introduce these two dishes in Mumbai was because the crowd there was more conscious about eating ghee (a major component of dal baati) as they viewed it as fattening, whereas in Ahmedabad, people didn't worry about it too much. Also, Mumbai being a cosmopolitan city, had a large population of the Marwari community (which tradionally made dal baati in their homes), and patra was served at many local establishments. Ahmedabad was traditionally a Gujarati city, so these two dishes weren't found a lot over there and people would go especially to Swati to eat it.

One woman remarked that she was grateful for this new branch because now, when she spoke to her sister-in-law in Mumbai, she could proudly say, "See, we have a Swati too!"

14

Moving On After Mistakes

MEANWHILE, WE CONTINUED WITH OUR CATERING business, both in Mumbai and for outstation orders, but it came with its own share of problems and mistakes. Though big mistakes were rare, they did happen occasionally and we had to learn how to deal with them.

One of the first mistakes I remember was when we had gone to cater a wedding function in Alibaug (a coastal town, south of Mumbai) in 2006. The ceremony was held in a bungalow and while the guests were on the first and second floors, we were set up in its compound. We were required to cater for around 200 people. We had previously undertaken catering orders for almost ten times the number of guests and it had always gone smoothly. This time, however, luck was not on our side and we made two mistakes.

The first mistake was in guessing the proportion of food that would be required by the guests. Catering works mainly on estimates, you estimate the number of people who will be there (because there are always last minute additions and dropouts), you estimate their taste and preferences, and you estimate their appetite for each item.

Now, we had already noted down the amount of ingredients we would require, but one cook forewarned us about over-ordering and said that a lot of food would get wasted. He appeared very confident about his prediction and insisted that we reduce the quantity by almost one-third. Since he seemed sure of himself, I went against my gut feeling and reduced the quantities ordered.

We had customised a colourful menu for the wedding, with starters that included *kand ka dahi vada* and topped with *kand ka sev*. The yam gave the dish its purple colour and made it look very attractive. For the main course, we created *green ponk rice* that was to be eaten with *masala kadhi*, and for dessert, we had *puran poli*.

The food started to run out almost immediately and many of the guests still hadn't been served. I panicked and asked the staff to try and find whatever ingredients they could in Alibaug itself and with those we tried making new recipes on the spot, just so that we would have something to serve the guests. This wasn't a fool proof plan, however, because everyone realised that we had underestimated the food required and were now cooking up recipes to cover up our blunder. Had we gone with the proportions I had estimated, we could have avoided this big embarrassment.

The second mistake, though not directly our fault, was regarding the staff. For catering orders we would usually hire the serving staff from third party companies, as most of our staff would be busy handling Swati. For the Alibaug wedding we did the same, but unknown to us, most of the regular senior staff from the service company was on leave. Instead of informing us, they sent newer, inexperienced staff in their place, thinking that they would manage.

The layout of the bungalow was such that the staff had to collect their trays from us in the compound and serve the food on the first and second floors. This required immense coordination and skills, to not only efficiently carry the food upstairs but also to make sure that every guest was served as they roamed around the expanse of the bungalow.

Being completely raw and untrained, the staff could not handle the food and the crowds, and caused many blunders. The food would not reach up on time. They would forget who had requested more of which dish, and they couldn't remember whom they had served and whom they hadn't. The caterer is responsible for all aspects of the food, including cooking and serving, so these mistakes by employees of the service company also reflected poorly on us.

We had done many bigger weddings before, but somehow this function was not a good day for us and we felt very disappointed with the mistakes we made.

Another example was a wedding we were asked to cater at a Parsi Fire Temple a few years later. Now, for Parsi wedding functions, the Fire Temple had a rule that while they supplied non-vegetarian caterers, for vegetarian food any outside caterers were allowed. We had catered wedding functions like this many times before, and this time, my dear friend had asked me to cater the function for her daughter's wedding.

It was a sit-down lunch and we were going to be serving our signature Gujarati cuisine with some variations. For starters I created a *Lucknow chaat* – a unique item that no one had tasted before. In the main course, we had *ponk muthiya vegetable* eaten with *masala roti*, and for desserts we had hot jalebis and hand-churned sitaphal or kesar pista ice creams.

Now, the usual service company that we used to book was unavailable, so we decided to hire another company that also had a good reputation. We were mindful about asking them to send us only their well-trained staff, keeping in mind the lessons we had learnt from our previous experience.

What we didn't realise until the service started was that while the servers were all well-trained, they had been trained only in the aspect of buffet lunches and had no experience with sit-down lunches. A buffet style meal is very different from one in which you have to serve the guests while they sit. There are a lot of nuances like which side to serve from, how much of each item to serve, how to arrange the food in someone's plate, how to move down the line from one guest to another; and these servers didn't know any of it.

They kept making mistakes, serving too much or too little, banging into each other, and being so clumsy that it cast a shadow over the whole experience. While the food was top-notch like always, no one could properly enjoy it as they were focusing on the servers. Towards the end of the function, I could hear people saying that "Asha's catering is not good" and it pained me deeply. Even my friend whose function it was and had invited me to cater it, didn't talk to me for many weeks afterwards because she was so upset with the service.

Eventually I realised that these ups and downs are a part of the business, and no matter how much you try to prevent them, sometimes they just happen. The best thing to do is to learn from such experiences and use them to make you and the restaurant stronger.

Family Album

Asha's father, Panalal Jhaveri

Asha's mother, Minakshi Jhaveri

Asha and her nani

Asha as a young woman

Asha at her painting exhibition with her mother

Asha and her brother, Anand

Asha's mother, Minakshi, was labeled as a 'Cookery Hostess' by Femina Magazine. Swati Snacks was also featured in the tourist book '$5 And $10 A Day In India' compiled by Air India and published in New York, as the article mentions.

MINAKSHI JHAVERI

The neat little kitchen in her apartment is a beehive of activity — with Minakshi Jhaveri trying out tempting pizzas, pungent pao-bhaji and a host of other dishes. She runs a profitable cafeteria "Swati Snacks" in Bombay where she sells bhel-puri, pani-puri and other snacks, besides, hand-churned ice-creams made from fresh fruits retaining their natural flavours as no colours or essences are used.

"Wholesome, home-prepared snacks at reasonable prices, made under hygienic conditions is what people want — and I give them what they want," smiled Minakshi. She also caters for wedding receptions and parties.

Having a business acumen she was keen to start something on her own. She discerned that catering would be profitable. "Extra income is always welcome—it would enable me to buy those extras and small luxuries for my children," she commented.

In those days, about 14 years ago, it needed considerable courage to overcome restraints imposed by a conservative society. "My major problem was to overcome social snobbery. Many scoffed at my idea, but I was determined. I realised that nothing was below one's dignity in one's own business — no matter what people said. But my mother kept an open mind vis a vis my decision." A beginning was made. She stepped into the business world in her own way by selling bhel, pani-puri and other snacks from her own residence. Initially she cooked all the delicacies herself. Within a short time when her business grew, she trained local cooks. Later, she thought of opening a cafeteria. Started more than a decade ago, "Swati Snacks" has made a steady progress, and has built a favourable reputation among the various classes of people in search of tasty, sumptuous snacks. Her personal supervision, her cheerful, jovial nature and a bit of public relations have made her a successful businesswoman.

Minakshi welcomes suggestions and complaints and is receptive to new ideas. A busy metropolis teems with particular and specialised demands therefore she has to introduce new items to cater to ever-varying tastes. "That is how I have started selling pizzas and pao-bhaji at the cafeteria."

Minakshi recommends this to any woman with time and plenty of energy. "Catering today offers ample scope to those interested in a useful career. One has to work hard but it gives joy and satisfaction and a sense of achievement. If women get together on such a project — nothing like it!" she maintains. "With an initial investment of a hundred rupees you can make a beginning from your own kitchen and see your business flourish!"

Familywise, Minakshi has no problems as her son and daughter are married. An exacting schedule of work does not subdue her manifold activities. She gives vent to her creative urge by doing hand-embroidery, knitting and crochet at which she is an expert.

MINAKSHI JAVERI

To the residents of the busy Tardeo locality, and for those who have heard the name, Swati books are a must. By now the name has acquired a special ring. Behind this small business, now a sizeable old, is energetic Minakshi Javeri. Her shop sells bhel-puri, pani-puri, and home-made ice-cream. "When I saw these tempts sold in Bombay in unclean surroundings, I got the idea for my little shop." Entirely supervised by Minakshi and managed with thrift, the place draws upper class clientele, people very particular about cleanliness. "Diligence pays. Hard work brings its own reward."

Any handicaps? "Yes," admitted Mrs. Javeri. "The non-availability of good, uniform, basic ingredients is my major handicap. Without this, quality is bound to suffer." And further: "Selective buying assures quality, and it is this side of my business which consumes most of my time."

Family-wise, Minakshi has no problems. Her children are all grown up, as the time adjustment is easy. "Now that the business is established and running smoothly, I have less work. It was full fourteen hours' hard toil, at the start."

Mrs. Javeri recommends this type of business to women with time and plenty of energy. "It is very satisfying to see people enjoy the fruits of your hard labour. Our evenings are full. The servers in the area are busy. Holidays and week-ends spell extra work, but then, it's all part of a good, flourishing business."

Perin Nicholson

ANASUYA SUMMANWAR   Minakshi Javeri   Anasuya Summanwar

EVE'S IN BUSINESS

Minakshi was also featured in The Times of India newspaper where she spoke about her journey on breaking the glass ceiling and becoming a successful woman business-owner in traditional India.

Swati Snacks

Asha at the reopening of a renovated Swati at Tardeo in 2000

Asha welcomed the famous Padma Shri, Padma Bhushan,
Padma Vibhushan, Yogacharya BKS Iyengar at Swati.
He was also named one of the 100 most influential people
in the world by Time Magazine in 2004.

Master Chef Viralalji:
One of the pillars of Swati Snacks

The eye-catching menu board made
Shyama and admired by custome

An inside look at the Swati Snacks restaurant at Tardeo on a regular day

Workforce Family

Asha with her restaurant staff outside the
Swati Snacks in Ahmedabad

Asha with her chefs and kitchen staff inside the
Swati Snacks kitchen in Ahmedabad

Awards

Asha receiving the Times Food Award for
Swati Snacks over the years

Signature Dishes

Some mouthwatering, landmark dishes at Swati Snacks
that are much loved by its regular customers

Bajri Uttapam

Bedai Roti, Alu Shak and Shrikhand

Satpadi Gatta

Thalipit Pitla

Baked Masala Khichdi

Paneer Lifafa

Panki

Falafel

Starters

Patra Samosa With Dhokla *(For 4 samosas)*

Ingredients • 1 *patra leaf* (colocasia / taro leaf)
• 1 bowl white dhokla *atta* (flour)
• ½ bowl sour curd • 2 tsp. oil • ½ tsp. Eno
fruit salt powder • 2 tbsp. tempura atta
• Salt and green chilli paste as per taste
• *Besan* (gram flour) and coriander chutney
as required • Oil for deep-frying

Method:

1. Wash the patra leaf and wipe it dry with
   a cloth

2. Cut the leaf into thin strips and set aside

3. Soak the white dhokla atta in sour curd for
   two hours and then add salt, oil, green chilli
   paste and Eno fruit salt powder to the mix

4. Pour the dhokla mix in a small plate and steam it for 20 minutes

5. After cooling, crumble the dhokla with your bare hands

6. Add green coriander chutney and a little curd to the crumbled dhokla and make
   small balls out of the mixture

7. In the strips of patra leaves, place the balls of dhokla and fold the strips into the
   shape of samosas

8. Seal any open portion with a paste of moist besan

9. Dip the samosas in a tempura atta mixture and deep-fry them

Patwadi Tart *(For 6 tarts)*

Ingredients • 1 bowl besan • 1 onion • 1 spring
onion • 6 tart shells • ½ tsp. garlic • ½ tsp. chilli
powder • ¼ tsp. garam masala • ½ lemon juice
• 1 tsp. oil • Few mustard seeds • *Sev* (small
pieces of crunchy noodles made from gram
flour) and coriander to garnish

Method:

1. Set aside small tart shells for this
   preparation

2. Roast besan on a slow fire and sieve it
   once it cools; then set it aside

3. Heat a little oil in a pan. Add mustard seeds
   and roast the chopped onion. Add garlic, salt, red
   chilli powder and garam masala, and then add water and bring the mixture to a boil

4. Reduce the heat, slowly add the roasted besan, and stir gently with a wooden spoon
   making sure no lumps remain; then add lemon juice and oil

5. Use part of this besan to make the gravy by adding water

6. Use the rest of the besan to make small balls

7. Place one ball in each tart shell; top it off with the gravy, sev, finely chopped spring
   onions and coriander leaves

Main Course

Val Dal Khichdi And Tandalja Bhaji Kadhi *(Serves 2)*

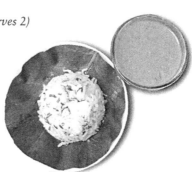

Ingredients For The Khichdi:
• 1 bowl rice • 1 tomato • 500 gm. onion
• ½ bowl *Val dal* (Lima beans lentils)
• 1 tbsp. ghee • ½ tsp. garlic • 2 sticks
cinnamon • 3 cloves • 3 tsp. lemon juice
• Pinch of turmeric, jeera and salt

For The Kadhi: • 1 bowl curd • 1 tsp.
besan • ½ a bunch of *tandalja bhaji* (also
known as Amarnath: a leafy vegetable)
• 1 tsp. chilli paste

Method: For The Khichdi:
1. Soak Val dal and rice together for two hours in a pot
2. Add water, turmeric, salt and cook to make a khichdi, and then let it cool
3. In a pan, roast finely chopped onions, tomato and garlic with ghee
4. In another pan, roast whole jeera, cinnamon sticks, garlic, and red chilli powder with ghee
5. Mix all of this with the khichdi and garnish with lemon juice and chopped coriander leaves

For The Kadhi:
6. Mix curd, besan and water with a hand mixer; then set aside
7. Chop the tandalja bhaji
8. In a pot, heat ghee and oil together, add jeera, garlic, salt, and chopped tandalja bhaji
9. Once the bhaji is cooked, add the kadhi (as made in step 6) and boil together; serve with the khichdi

Paneer Rice With Tuvar Dal Amti *(Serves 2)*

Ingredients For The Paneer Rice:
• 1 bowl rice • ½ bowl paneer • 1 tsp. ghee
• 1tsp. jeera • ½ tsp. green chilli paste
• 1 tsp. lemon juice

For Tuvar Dal Amti:
• ½ bowl *Tuvar dal* (Harhar dal / Pigeon
peas lentils) • 2 tsp. ghee • ½ bowl
chopped onion • ½ bowl green chutney
• Coriander, lemon, ginger, garlic,
cinnamon, cloves, *chana daliya* (made from
chickpeas), chilli paste as per taste

Method: For The Paneer Rice:
1. Soak the rice for two hours, add salt and cook
2. Chop medium-sized pieces of paneer
3. In a pan, heat ghee and add jeera, garlic, green chilli paste; then add the paneer pieces
4. Add this paneer to the rice in a plate and top it off with coriander leaves and lemon juice

For Tuvar Dal Amti:
5. Wash and cook Tuvar dal in a cooker and then grind it with a hand mixer
6. In a pot, heat ghee and add chopped onions, garlic, cinnamon, cloves, and green coriander chutney, chana daliya, lemon, ginger, and green chilli, and roast all of it well
7. Add it to the Tuvar dal mixture and heat it well; then add lemon juice and salt to taste

Desserts

Green Peas Puran Poli Recipe *(3 Puran Polis)*

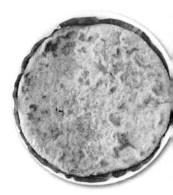

Ingredients For The Stuffing:
• 2 bowls raw green peas • ½ bowl sugar
• 5 tsp. ghee • ½ tsp. cardamom

For The Roti:
• 1 bowl wheat flour • 2 tsp. ghee • 1 tbsp. milk • Rice flour as required

Method:

1. Grind fresh green peas in a mixer without adding water to it

2. Heat ghee in a pan and roast the green peas in it

3. Add sugar to the roasted mixture

4. Once the moisture from the sugar dries up and the ghee is visible, remove the pan from the stove and add ground cardamom

6. Knead the dough for the rotis with wheat flour, ghee and milk

7. Roll out small rotis, put some of the green peas mixture in the centre, and fold it like a *kachori* (stuffed puri)

8. Roll it out flat, now to a larger size, with rice flour

9. Roast the roti over a low flame and remove when golden brown

10. Coat the rotis lightly with some ghee and serve

Ponkh No Shiro *(Serves 2)*

Ingredients • 2 bowls *ponk* (tender jowar or sorghum) • 3 tbsp. ghee • ½ tsp. cardamom • ½ bowl sugar • 6 peeled almonds

Method:

1. Wash raw ponk thoroughly to remove any dirt or stains

2. Grind it lightly in a mixer, but do not grind it into a paste

3. In a pot, heat ghee and roast the ponk for a short period of time

4. Add milk, and when the milk gets dissolved, add sugar

5. Heat it over a slow flame until the sugar is burnt

6. Take the pot off the burner and top it off with almond flakes and ground cardamom

15

The Life In Your Years

IN 2006 WE RECEIVED NEWS THAT SEEMED TO MOVE THE
very ground underneath our feet. Neel, now a young man
of 30 years, was diagnosed with leukaemia. He had a
family of his own, with his daughter only four years old at
that time. After the initial shock and heartbreak, we knew
we would do whatever it took to give Neel a fighting
chance at life. Anand, Neel, Shaan and their whole family
shifted to Singapore so that Neel could get access to the
best healthcare and doctors.

Their architecture business was temporarily suspended
and the staff was instructed to look after Swati. It was one
of the most challenging periods that we as a family had
to go through, and the staff that had grown up with Neel,
immediately stepped up to their new roles as managers.
They put in long hours, and went beyond their duties to
make sure that Swati could keep running smoothly. They
purchased the raw materials, cooked the food, and dealt
with customers. Over the next three years, they proved

that Swati was their baby and that nothing is too much when it comes to family. It felt exactly like the olden days when Viralalji and others had stepped up to handle Swati after my mother's demise.

In 2008, despite all our efforts, Neel passed away. There are no words to describe what that loss felt like, but slowly and steadily the family shifted back to Ahmedabad and we all started to pick up the pieces of our lives.

When I think about him one quote comes to mind, "It's not the years of life that count, it's the life in your years." For as long as I have known them, Shaan and Neel lived a life that was uniquely their own, and through their words and actions they beautified the lives of everyone they came in contact with. For me, they will always be little boys running around the kitchen in Swati, asking Viralalji to teach them some recipes. Watching them as they grew up from mischievous boys to smart young men has been one of the greatest joys and privileges of my life.

16

The Path Finds You

FROM 1986 TO 2011, I HAD BEEN AN ARDENT FOLLOWER of Lord Shiva who I was introduced to by my yoga teacher. In 2011, I came across a tape recording of the *Shrimad Bhagwat Katha* and was taken in by the words, which resonated very strongly with me. After a few months, I took a trip to Vrindavan (a historical city in the Mathura district of Uttar Pradesh), which was said to be Lord Krishna's birthplace. Over there I came across a very renowned *pundit* who was famous for his recitation of the katha. I requested him to come with me to my home in Mumbai and recite the katha there. He agreed and within a few months we made the necessary arrangements for his travel and stay.

After hearing his recitation of the katha, I knew that there was something very powerful in his voice and that more people should have a chance to experience it. With this in mind, I spoke to my friends and relatives who I knew would be interested in an event like this and asked them to accompany me to a place called Shukratal (an ancient city in the state of Uttarakhand), 100km away from Haridwar, where the Bhagwat katha was traditionally recited. We requested the same pundit to accompany us, and sitting on the banks of the river, I was charmed once again by his melodious, magnetic voice. Back home, I continued to recite the katha and spent many evenings listening to the recorded audio play on loop.

In 2013, I came across the book, 'The Power Of Now', by Eckhart Tolle. It was my first introduction to spirituality away from religion, and it changed my perspective. It showed me a new way to live, behave, and act. The book played such a pivotal role in my life that immediately after completing it, I signed up for a week's retreat with Eckhart Tolle in Australia. The retreat helped broaden my understanding about spirituality and shifted me from idol worship to the path of self-realisation.

Back in Mumbai, I looked for the publisher who had brought out such a revolutionary book in India and came across Yogi Impressions. On an impulse, I called them up and asked to meet Gautam who was the head of the publishing house. For two months there was no response and then one day, out of the blue, I got a call saying that I could meet Gautam at his residence at Churchgate on the following Sunday morning. His house was only a 15-minute drive from mine and I immediately agreed.

Much to my surprise, Gautam was much younger than I thought. He was almost 25 years younger than me but had wisdom that surpassed his age. We spent around an hour together, during which we spoke about The Power Of Now and he explained various aspects of *Advaita* to me, especially its impact on daily living. I enjoyed our conversation thoroughly, and invited him to meet me for coffee one day so that we could continue our conversation. Over the next few months, we would meet often and I started to gain deep insights into the path of spirituality and self-discovery.

A Loss And A Milestone

In 2011, 47 years after Swati first started, Viralalji retired. He was well into his eighties by then and had been a pillar of Swati since its inception. The restaurant had been as much his baby as it was our mother's and he had raised it lovingly. He had also been a father figure to Anand and me while growing up, especially after we lost our mother, and had been a prominent part of Shaan and Neel's life as well. The ambience of Swati was unimaginable without him, but we knew it was time for him to move on.

With a bittersweet feeling in our hearts, we bid adieu to him as he boarded the train to his village. I had given him a lump sum amount when he left, though I knew fully well that his service to Swati and to our family could never be repaid. Over the next two years, I visited him in his village often, taking food and news from Mumbai, eager to gain his insights on matters, and he was always welcoming towards me.

By 2013, Viralalji had aged considerably and it was taking a toll on him. When, in July, the news came of his death, we were prepared. I knew that he had lived a full, rich life and that his time was simply up. Repeating this thought in my mind, I reached his village to say goodbye to the man who had been a father and mentor to me.

In 2014, we celebrated 50 years since the inception of Swati. We hosted a small, intimate lunch buffet where we invited friends, family, and our most loyal customers at the Tardeo outlet of Swati – the place where it all began. I decided to create a special, customised menu for the occasion since most guests would have frequently eaten from the regular menu. We served *pat wadi rasa,* and *vatana-batata rotlo* as starters, items like *chole ka saag* with *masala puri* for the main course, and our unique *strawberry shrikand* for dessert. Later on, we also hosted another party for the staff where we gave them tokens of appreciation to express our gratitude towards their loyal service.

The year was a high for us and especially for me. I had never imagined that we would be able to reach so far and have such a great impact on people by offering simple homely food prepared by simple people. The year filled us with confidence and pride and we were ready to take Swati to its next 50 years.

My Spiritual Search Ends

Around this time, in 2014, one of my friends gave me a book called 'The Eight Spiritual Breaths' which was based on the ancient practice of *Brahmavidya* and consisted of eight different breathing exercises. My friend had received the book from her cousin and thought that I would really like it. I flipped through the book but wasn't interested in getting into such a deep practice, so instead of reading it, I put it aside on my shelf and promptly forgot about it.

A few months later, I got a call from that same friend's cousin and she inquired if I had read the book. I apologised and tried explaining, but she waved it off, saying that she could make me meet the author in case I wanted to know more about it. I readily agreed and we made a plan to visit the author the following Sunday.

Much to my surprise, I was led to the same house where Gautam lived. The author of the book was Santosh Sachdeva, who was Gautam's mother and a spiritual Guru! All this time I had been meeting Gautam and I had never known about his mother. My curiosity about the Breaths and about her was piqued and I asked her to teach me the practice. She guided me to her disciple, Rohit Arya, who used to teach the Breaths, since she had stopped teaching them herself a while ago.

Rohit and I would meet once a week at my house, learn the practice of the Breaths and then meditate together. Our time together gave me an opportunity to tap into his vast reserves of knowledge about rituals, traditions, and spiritual practices in India. During one of our conversations, he mentioned that he used to go for a *girivalam* to the Arunachala hill that was regarded as the embodiment of Shiva at Tiruvannamalai – a three-hour drive from the city of Chennai in South India. Situated at its base was the ashram of the famous Advaita sage Sri Ramana Maharshi. The girivalam was a 13km walk around the hill that was said to destroy past *karmas*. Since I was always ready to try out new things, I decided to accompany him the next time he went.

I took my first trip to Arunachala with Rohit and Gautam in 2015. It took me around four hours to complete the circumambulation. During one part of the girivalam, we passed through the neighbouring market place. From there I could see Arunachala rising tall above the crowds and I remember looking at it and not being able to see a mountain – I could only see Lord Shiva's face. That visual stayed with me throughout that girivalam and even once we were back in Mumbai. It kept drawing me back to itself and for the next year, I went every month to Arunachala with Rohit to do a girivalam and to see Lord Shiva's face again.

In 2016 I had gone to meet Santosh Ma to talk about my journey with The Eight Spiritual Breaths and she invited me to start coming to her residence for group meditation on Wednesdays and Thursdays, where other students of the course and her disciples would come together. I started regularly attending those sessions, and coupled with my daily practice of the Breaths, I started to feel as if I was reborn. I don't say this sentence lightly; I truly believe that the Breaths and my Guru (I later recognised Santosh Sachdeva as my Guru) changed my life.

The most tangible result of the Breaths was the level of discipline it brought to my life. Doing the one and a half hour long practice every morning, whether rain or shine, workday or holiday, transformed my perspective on the meaning of the words 'dedication' and 'consistency'. Even when I would go for holidays, I would take a separate room so that I could wake up early in the morning and practice the Breaths peacefully. That level of commitment started to reflect in all other work I would take up in my life too.

The introspection and meditation helped me to become more accepting of others. Initially, I would frequently get upset over the habits or flaws in my husband or friends, but through my practice, I learnt that everyone has their own journey and it is not my job to change or judge them. This realisation helped all my relationships become smoother and happier.

Another major change it brought was in the way I dealt with my emotions. I used to have a bad temper and would frequently scream at the staff for their mistakes. I would think that that was the only way to keep them in check. The Affirmations (positive visualisations) recited after each Breath made me realise that since there was no one 'lesser' than me, I had no right to look down on my staff or think of them as people needing to be kept in line. Once I let go of my desire to control them and prevent mistakes before they happened, I gave the staff space and freedom to automatically become the best versions of themselves. This change was appreciated by my staff who would say that I was like a new, better boss for all of them, and their words made me feel very proud of how far I had come.

Looking back, I can see how life led me first to Gautam and then to Santosh Ma, and how my lifelong search for the Divine ended at the feet of my Guru. Each stage of my spiritual journey, and the changes it brought in me, were reflected in my interactions with the staff and customers at Swati. The more I grew personally, the more Swati was able to grow with me.

17

Looking Towards The Future

TILL 2016, WE HAD ONE SWATI AT TARDEO, MUMBAI, and another at Law Garden, Ahmedabad. The Mumbai Swati was packed on most days and the people queuing up outside the restaurant would sometimes have to wait for one and a half hours just to get a seat inside. I never liked seeing people wait out in the rains or heat and knew we had to find a place to expand.

I suggested the idea of expansion to Anand and thought that we could open one outlet in the suburbs. Since we already had one outlet in South Mumbai, I thought this would help us expand our customer base. But Anand was against the idea, as he knew that travelling between the two locations every day would get very tiring for me. He proposed opening the other outlet also in South Mumbai so that travelling would be easier and it would help distribute the crowd between the two places and cut down on waiting time.

Finding a space in South Mumbai that is big enough to accommodate 80 people and reasonably priced is difficult, and it took us almost eight months of looking before we chanced upon a place at Nariman Point – a business district of Mumbai. We started work on the restaurant, with Anand supervising the construction and design, and I looked at the practical aspects of opening a new branch.

We decided that the kitchen near the Tardeo outlet would be used as the central kitchen where all bases (such as the pani of pani puri) would be prepared and sent to both outlets every morning. The actual preparation of food (such as making hot pankis or dosas) would take place in the outlets independently. Every morning, we sampled the food at one outlet, and once the required changes were made, we called up the other location and asked them to make the same changes so that consistency of taste and quality was maintained across both restaurants.

While there were many problems we could avert because of our previous experience, there were others that we couldn't foresee. For example, the fact that offices would start shifting out of Nariman Point and relocate to Bandra Kurla Complex (an upcoming business district in the suburbs); or that, since we were surrounded in a business district, our sales during the afternoon would be less since everyone would be holed up in their offices; or that the construction of the Metro Transport System would barricade the road right outside our restaurant, making it difficult for people to get access to us.

These developments in the locality and surrounding community took us by surprise, but having more than 50 years of experience, we were much calmer and resilient in the face of these disadvantages. We introduced measures like 'happy hours' in which customers could get a discount on food items during the off-peak hours of the day, partnered with food delivery applications, introduced 'combo offers', and did all we could to make the best out of the situation. Gradually, crowds started to get drawn to this new outlet and we managed to have a steady stream of customers even on weekdays.

Tests Of Faith

While there are ups-and-downs in all environments that we can learn to adapt to, sometimes there are situations that make it seem as if we are spiralling right down to the depths of despair.

Initially, when the Coronavirus pandemic started, my reaction was the same as pretty much everyone else's – I thought it was just a stronger version of the flu that would soon disappear automatically. Even when the first lockdown took place in March 2020, I thought that the government was wisely being overprotective and that we would be 'back to normal' in three weeks.

One and a half years later – and still in lockdown – I know that I, like the rest of the world, severely underestimated the virus and the devastating impact it would have on families as well as businesses worldwide.

Besides the tragic loss of human lives, our livelihoods

have also taken a strong beating – businesses were thrown into losses or even shut down completely, and many people lost their jobs.

Few businesses have been as hard hit as the restaurant and catering services. Last year when few of the lockdown restrictions eased and home delivery of food was allowed, the situation improved to an extent. However, food delivery applications and services accounted for less than 10% of our revenue. Though we were incurring losses, I didn't want to leave our staff to fend for themselves during these turbulent times. We paid them 60% of their full salary throughout the pandemic, even though they were not working. For this, we had to dip heavily into our savings to compensate our workforce across two cities and four branches of Swati Snacks.

Soon the orders kept picking up, but we were still short of what we needed to break even. Even as lockdown restrictions eased further towards the end of 2020 and restaurants could open with limited capacities, people were still hesitant to step out of their homes, particularly for outdoor dining. It took a few months for people's confidence to increase, and just as we had started to feel hopeful about the situation, the second lockdown hit us in April 2021 and we were once again forced to close our doors.

Moreover, in the middle of this global catastrophe, I also had a personal health crisis to deal with. In June 2020, I was diagnosed with a severe illness. After I got over the initial reaction, I vowed to myself that I would get through this. My deep roots of spirituality and prayer held me firm and I started to look at the illness as a test of my faith; I knew that while my body was in the hands of the best doctors, my mind and emotions were solely mine to deal with and strengthen. And the more I surrendered to the Universe, the more the Universe opened itself to me.

Armed with a positive attitude, I strode into every appointment, I held the hand of God through every session, and went to bed at night in the arms of life – it was a journey unlike any other, but I am now stronger, healthier, happier and more blessed than I've ever been.

I do not know when the pandemic will end or how long will it take for the world to completely heal. But I know that how we deal with loss and pain in our life today will shape who we, all of humanity, will be tomorrow. This pandemic, like my illness, is a test of our faith, patience and perseverance; we may not have chosen to take this test but we can choose to ace it and come out on the other side with our spirits intact.

There are a few practices that have helped me stay mentally, emotionally and physically fit during the lockdown. Even though the restaurant was closed and I had the flexibility of time, I used to wake up early in the morning to exercise, practice my pranayama and meditate. I would also ensure that I was eating healthy, hearty meals at home thrice a day to prevent myself from snacking or binge eating due to stress and boredom. In addition to these, I decided to switch off the television set and discontinue newspapers – since I thought they were too full of negativity – and turn my attention to reading lots of books, particularly spiritual ones.

The past year simultaneously made me feel the strongest and most vulnerable I've ever felt. I can now say that I *know* myself and everything I am capable of. And this is what gives me hope: If my personal pain could bring me to a place of so much love and light, then maybe this collective suffering on earth will make us all part of a brighter, happier world one day.

A Story Of Hope And Joy

In the half a century that we have been in business, a lot of things have changed. Nuclear families with working couples have made it harder to cook food at home. People have started to eat out a lot more as compared to my childhood. They are also exposed to a wide variety of cuisines, cultures, and crave different food every night instead of the staple 'roti-sabzi'. Many people prefer buying ready-to-eat meals or eating take-out instead of the hassle of hiring someone to cook daily. The palate of younger generations is also changing and they no longer want heavy food. They are calorie-conscious, health-conscious and want food that helps them attain their fitness goals.

At Swati we constantly upgrade old recipes to make them healthier and tastier while keeping our diverse customers in mind. We have traditional, home-cooked recipes for our loyal customers and keep inventing new recipes like *paneer lifafa* for those craving uniqueness.

We have also added our own twists to standard dishes such as, in the Falafel, instead of tahini sauce we use *til ka sauce* and we top it with cabbage, finely chopped spinach and small fried falafel patties made of moong dal. We create funky new inventions for children like *chocolate dosas* and design health-conscious options for the youth like *bajra-paneer pizza, bajra uttapam, jowar bhel* and *chola methi dhokla.* The crowd at Swati is always a mix of people of all ages and communities, and this makes me very happy, as we are able to attract the younger generation while also adhering to our traditional roots.

At the time when I took over Swati, hardly any women would work professionally. Today, I am glad to see that times are changing and women are rising up to claim their rightful place in society. I believe that whether you are a mother, doctor, teacher or chef, it should be because you want to be one, not because society forces or limits you to it.

There are many fad diets that spring up from time to time, asking you to eat no fat or all fat or some other strict combination. I haven't personally tried any so I don't know if they work, but I do believe in being conscious of what one eats and of exercising regularly. I do my yoga practice and Breaths regularly, and try to eat food that keeps me feeling light and fit. From time to time, I also love eating fried food or sweet dishes. Life is to be enjoyed – with friends, family and yourself.

Food is more than a necessity, it is an expression of love, tradition and culture, and it is wonderful to indulge in it from time to time.

A typical day in my life involves waking up at 5 a.m. to practice The Eight Spiritual Breaths and then sitting for half an hour of meditation. I also practice yoga thrice a week under the guidance of my teacher. Around 11 a.m., I go to Swati to taste the food and make the alterations. My afternoons are spent in a meeting or at the restaurant, after which I come home for a short rest. In the evening, once a week, I go for meditation at my Guru's home or for an outing with friends or family.

My food starts with a cup of green tea and *khakra* at 7 a.m. Then I have a big glass of spinach and kale juice at 9 a.m. along with five almonds, two walnuts, and two dates. Lunch is at 1 p.m. with at least one portion of green vegetables, one dal and different rotis made from jowar, moong or bajri. In the afternoon, I have a cup of hot *masala chai* at 4.30 p.m. along with khakra, and end my day with a dinner of spinach or *doodhi soup* and items such as *moong dal chila* or *dal dhokli* and lots of vegetables like spinach, carrots, and green peas.

On Saturday nights I usually go for dinner with my friends to different clubs such as CCI, NSCI, Malabar Hill Club, etc., and once a week, I eat lunch outside with a relative or friend. When we eat out, I enjoy exploring new cuisines and sampling the signature dishes at each restaurant that we go to. I think this spirit of adventure is very important because one never knows when one will end up having the 'best meal' or 'best dish' of one's life.

Every few months, I take a trip to Tiruvannamalai, Pondicherry, or other cities in India. I enjoy visiting *ashrams* and ancient temples, so many of my visits are to places in South India, which hosts a lot of India's cultural treasures. Once in a while I also take a leisure vacation to destinations outside India with some friends or relatives. Recently I have also started cutting back at work and devoting extra time to reading books or just enjoying life.

I never had a chance to ask my mother what Swati means, but I think, through life, I discovered it. In Hinduism, the name 'Swati' means the brightest star – and like all stars do, when my life was at its darkest after the loss of my mother and the sudden, unexpected inheritance of the restaurant, that was when I rose up and shone the brightest.

Looking back at my school, childhood and early marriage days, I know that no one could have guessed that the shy, fearful girl I was would one day be the proud owner of a chain of successful restaurants in India.

Life has been an exciting adventure with a lot of unexpected twists and turns and bumps along the way. Through it all, I have watched myself grow professionally, personally, and spiritually in every possible way. I have found friends in strangers, help in unexpected places, and courage in my darkest moments.

If nothing else, my life is a story of 'hope' when all seems lost, and 'joy' makes the pain worthwhile: It is a story of a little girl called Asha and her younger brother Anand, discovering the bittersweet flavours of life.

Acknowledgements

I would like to thank my brother Anand, who encouraged me to continue our mother's legacy; master chef Viralal Maharaj, who mentored and supported me throughout this journey; the entire staff at Swati, for their loyalty and dedication, and my family, friends, and loyal customers. I shall always be grateful for their love and affection.

Glossary

Aarti – a Hindu ceremony in which lights are lit and offered up to gods

Asanas – postures adopted in yoga

Advaita – non duality

Aloo ki sukhi sabzi – potatoes cooked with simple masalas (mixtures of ground spices) like red chilli powder and haldi (turmeric powder)

Ashram – a hermitage, monastic community, or other place of religious retreat

Bajra paneer pizza – the pizza base is made of bajra instead of maida, and topped with paneer instead of cheese

Bajra uttapam – made from bajra aata (millet) and boiled bajri instead of rice aata, and baked with toppings into a pancake

Bhaiyyas – a pejorative term for migrant workers from the northern states of Uttar Pradesh and Bihar

Bhindi ki sabzi – ladyfingers made with dhaniya (cumin) powder, red chillies, haldi and salt

Bidai – ritual of the bride bidding farewell to her family

Brahmavidya – knowledge of creation

Bread-dhokla – made by roasting cumin and other masalas in a pan, adding curd and the chopped bread pieces

Bua – paternal aunt

Chaat masala – a popular spice mix that has a tangy flavour

Chaats – savoury snacks

Chashni – liquid sugar

Chawl – concrete structures divided into separate tenements offering basic accommodation

Chocolate dosas – made with generous amounts of Nutella paste

Chola – a dry pulse

Chola methi dhokla – made from chola dal (chickpeas) with lots of methi (fenugreek) and steamed, instead of rice and urad dal aata (black gram)

Chole ka saag – a vegetable made from chickpeas

Churma ladoo – made from wheat, jaggery and covered with poppy seeds

Churros – made out of deep fried corn flour and served with chocolate dip

Dahi puri – puri (a small, round piece of bread made of unleavened wheat flour, deep fried) with potato filling, meethi chutney (a cold sauce made from date and tamrinds) and curd, topped with moong (mung bean), red chilli powder and garnished with coriander

Dahi vadas – an Indian dish consisting of a ball made from mung bean pulses and deep fried, then topped with curd and meethi chutney

Dal baati – the dal is made out of moong dal, the baati is made out of wheat and ghee, and then baked

Dal dhokli – made out of chilke wali dal (unpolished pulses) and lots of vegetables like spinach, carrots, and green peas

Dhoklas – a dish made from gram flour and cooked by steaming

Doodhi – a vegetable made with boiled bottle gourd and basic masalas

Doodhi soup – boiled bottle gourd soup

Dosa – a rice pancake, originating in South India, made from fermented batter of rice and black gram

Drumstick ki sabzi – drumsticks coated with besan (gram flour) and yogurt, and cooked till thick

Enchiladas – a Mexican dish that is stuffed with spinach and cottage cheese, dipped in a red sauce, topped with cheese and baked to perfection

Fada ni khichree – a dish of tapioca pearls made with potatoes and peanuts

Gatte ka saag – made of small besan (gram flour) dumplings and put in a besan kadhi

Ghee – butter, clarified by boiling, used in Indian cooking

Girivalam – the practice of circling a sacred mountain or hill

Golas – made of ice, water and a sharbat (syrup) that rendered different colours to the golas

Golawala – ice candy seller

Green ponk rice – ponk is a green-coloured grain made out of wheat, and is seasonal to winter

Gujarati khatta-meetha dal – a dish traditional to the Gujarati community where pulses are cooked to taste sour and sweet

Gujarati toor dal – a type of pulse traditional to the Gujarati community

Gunda – a sticky summer vegetable made with coconut, coriander and basic masalas

Jalebis – a popular dessert in many parts of India, they are syrup-filled rings that are deep fried

Jowar bhel – made from a grain called jowar (sorghum) which replaces the usual fried ingredients of sev (an Indian snack consisting of long, thin strands of gram flour, deep fried and spiced) and puris

Kadai – a bowl-shaped frying pan with two handles used in Indian cooking

Kali dal – black pulse

Kand ka dahi vada – vada made of yam (seasonal to winter) served with fresh curd, chutney, and masalas

Kand ka sev – made by boiling yam, cutting and then deep frying it

Karela – bitter gourd sweetened with jaggery

Karmas – the force created by a person's actions that are believed in Hinduism and Buddhism to determine what that person's next life will be like. Dissolving of karmas is supposed to be the way to enlightenment

Kesar pista – saffron and pistachios

Khakra – a Gujarati version of tortilla/crisp bread, made with flour, spices, ghee, and lentils

Khaman dhokla – visually similar to cake made from a batter of gram flour cooked by steaming and served with green chutney

Lapsi – an auspicious Diwali dish made out of beaten wheat, with jaggery or sugar

Lucknow chaat – puris topped with moong dal bhajiya (lentil fritters), different chutneys, curd and chaat masalas

Maharaj – traditionally, a term of respect used for Hindu Brahmin cooks

Malai – a type of clotted cream originating in the Indian subcontinent, made by heating non-homogenised whole milk and allowing it to cool

Malpua – fried pancakes flavoured with fennel and cardamom and dunked in sugar syrup

Masala chai – a flavoured tea beverage made by brewing black tea with a mixture of aromatic Indian spices and herbs

Masala kadhi – thick gravy made with different spices

Masala puri – deep fried Indian bread

Masala roti – a flat round Indian bread cooked on a griddle and stuffed with moong dal masala

Matti ka kullad – mud tumblers/bowls

Meethi dal – sweetened pulses cooked like a gravy

Missal pav – a gravy made out of chickpeas, potatoes, chutney, curd, masalas and coriander, and served with bread

Moong dal chila – pancakes made from mung bean pulses

Moong ka kadhi – a type of pulse made from mung bean

Namkeens – salty snacks

Nana-nani – maternal grandparents

Navkar Mantra – one of the most important shlokas in Jainism through which we pay our homage to the Panch Parameshti (who are considered to be the Five Supreme deities).

Onion kulcha – maida roti (flat bread) garnished with onions and chillies

Orange basundi – made out of boiled thickened milk with fresh orange slices on top

Pakoda kadhi – a gravy with fritters inside it

Paneer lifafa – made from a big roti of maida (flour), cubes of roasted paneer (cottage cheese), masalas, and then folded like an envelope before roasting it

Pani puri – fried rava puris with spicy pudina pani (mint water), meetha chutney on the side, and an aloo-moong-chana (potato-mung bean-chickpeas) mixture

Panki – a famous Gujarati recipe made of rice, urad dal flour (black gram) and curd

Papads – thin, crisp disc-shaped snack typically based on a seasoned dough usually made from peeled black gram flour (urad flour), fried or cooked with dry heat.

Pat wadi rasa – a Maharashtrian chaat where besan is cooked with masalas, spread in a plate, then cut it into small diamonds, and topped with a besan gravy

Patra – a type of paan (betal leaves) on which you put besan, masalas, and then fold and steam it

Pav bhaji – buttery roasted bread served with moderately spicy mix of mashed vegetables made from tomatoes, potatoes, green peas, onion, garlic, and special bhaji masala

Ponk muthiya vegetable – a vegetable gravy of boiled ponk with methi muthiya (made from chickpea flour and fenugreek)

Prasad – a devotional offering made to a god, typically consisting of food that is later shared among devotees.

Pudina paratha – tandoori wheat roti with stuffed pudina (mint)

Pundit – a Hindu scholar

Puran poli – made out of toor dal (a type of pulse), stuffed with jaggery, and then roasted

Puri – a small, round piece of bread made of unleavened wheat flour, deep fried and served with meat or vegetables.

Ragda patties – ragda is a light gravy made out of chickpeas, patties are made from potatoes, stuffed with green peas, and roasted

Raita – curd with masalas

Ramcharitmanas – an epic poem about the deeds of Lord Ram

Roti – Indian flat bread

Rudra puja – one of the greatest Vedic pujas (rituals) dedicated to Lord Shiva

Sambhar – a spicy south Indian dish consisting of lentils and vegetables

Sambhariya potatoes – a dry vegetable dish of potatoes made with coconut, coriander, and spices

Samosas – a triangular savory pastry fried in ghee or oil, containing spiced vegetables or meat

Satpadi roti – a roti comprised of seven layers and filled with masalas, with each individual layer visible

Sev puri – fried, flat, maida (flour) puris topped with aloo (potatoes), chutney, chopped onions, and coriander

Shiro – a sweet preparation made from mung lentils

Shlokas – prayers

Shrikhand – an Indian sweet dish of strained yogurt

Shrimad Bhagwat Katha – a katha (ancient text) of Lord Krishna

Sithaphal – custard apple

Skin potatoes – baby potatoes cooked with tomatoes, red chilli powder and other masalas

Strawberry shrikand – made from hung yogurt and sugar and flavoured with strawberries.

Tacos – a Mexican dish made from corn flour shells, filled with beans, cabbage, avocados, sour cream, green and red sauce, and topped with lot of cheese

Til dhoklas – a food, visually similar to cake made from a batter of gram flour (from chickpeas), cooked by steaming, and seasoned with sesame seeds

Til ka sauce – sauce made from sesame seeds

Undhiya – a mixed vegetable winter dish

Val ni dal – a semi-dry curry made from val (lima beans)

Vatana-batata rotlo – patties made from green peas and potatoes, roasted with masalas, and topped with fresh coconut milk

Vegetable do pyaza – a gravy made from potatoes, onions and other vegetables

White dhoklas – made out of rice, urad dal flour (black gram) and served with green chutney

White mava peda – an easy and simple to make Indian dessert made with evaporated milk solids and sugar

Yellow peda – similar to the white peda but with saffron

The author may be contacted on email:
jhaveriasha@gmail.com

For further details, contact:
Yogi Impressions LLP
1711, Centre 1, World Trade Centre,
Cuffe Parade, Mumbai 400 005, India.

Fill in the Mailing List form on our website
and receive, via email, information on
books, authors, events and more.
Visit: www.yogiimpressions.com

Telephone: (022) 2215 0207, 2215 5036
E-mail: yogi@yogiimpressions.com

 Join us on Facebook:
www.facebook.com/yogiimpressions

 Join us on Instagram:
www.instagram.com/yogi_impressions

ALSO PUBLISHED BY YOGI IMPRESSIONS

The Sacred India Tarot
Inspired by Indian Mythology and Epics

78 cards + 4 bonus cards + 350 page handbook

The Sacred India Tarot is truly an offering from India to the world. It is the first and only Tarot deck that works solely within the parameters of sacred Indian mythology – almost the world's only living mythology today.